Snap Out of It Now!

Snap Out of It Now!

FOUR STEPS TO INNER JOY

Adrianne Ahern, Ph.D.

SENTIENT PUBLICATIONS, LLC

A paperback original

Cover design by Kim Johansen, Black Dog Design
Book design by Nicholas Cummings
Cover photo by Jeremiah Sullivan

Library of Congress Cataloging-in-Publication Data

Ahern, Adrianne, 1960-
    Snap out of it now : four steps to inner joy / Adrianne Ahern.
        p. cm.
    ISBN 978-1-59181-056-8
    1. Joy. 2. Self-actualization (Psychology) I. Title.

BF575.H27A34 2007
158—dc22

2006029942

Printed in the United States of America

10 9 8 7 6 5 4 3 2 1

SENTIENT PUBLICATIONS

A Limited Liability Company
1113 Spruce Street
Boulder, CO 80302
www.sentientpublications.com

*To my late beloved father, Joseph Ahern,
and to my beautiful mother, Joyce Reeves Ahern.
I feel your love each day of my life.*

CONTENTS

Foreword by James Arthur Ray

W e live in exciting, accelerating times. In the last year, the smash hit book and movie The Secret, in which I'm a featured expert, has done more for the personal growth movement than anything in recent memory. People worldwide are embracing the Law of Attraction and racing past their old limiting beliefs and patterns. I've witnessed a dramatic shift, a visible quickening in the faces of the attendees in my Harmonic Wealth seminars. For many, the transformation has been swift and profound-creating a tangible giddy euphoria that has critics on the other side of the equation positively dumbfounded, even crying foul. Can you really catapult your life into the stratosphere simply by focusing on what you want? Can it really be so simple?

Yes. But it's hard for some people to achieve that focus, and I'll explain why in a moment. I can say with absolute certainty that the Law of Attraction does indeed work, which is why I've been teaching its principles-and other equally powerful ones-for the last two decades. But what about those people who have applied the techniques in The Secret, who've diligently followed the positive-thinking messages of the New Age movement for years, and yet are still struggling? Maybe you're one of them.

Maybe you've wondered why some people live in what appears to be a constant state of joy, love, and abundance, while others-perhaps you-feel left out of the party, strait-jacketed by unpredictable moods and self-defeating behaviors. Why do some people seem to be plagued by good old-fashioned bad vibes?

The real secret, one that world-renowned sports psychologist Dr. A knows well and lets you in on in this book (and has used with her top performance athletes for years) is that your body has its own little secret. As hard though it is to imagine, you're not always on your own side! No matter how positive you are, no matter how strong your will, your body is controlled by your unconscious mind, period. A mind with an agenda all of its own-and not always a positive one. Not so sure? Just think of your growing years. Experience any negative social conditioning back in your childhood? Is it so farfetched to think that those formative experiences remain-like a software program on your computer that, though you think you deleted it, continues running strong in the background?

I want you to take a minute to really sit with the idea that your mind might be undermining your will. That's a big statement. Your unconscious thoughts, beliefs, and feelings are more powerful than your will power. No matter what you think you're thinking, if your unconscious programming wants you to fail-to eat that whole carton of ice cream, or show up repeatedly late for work, or wrench your back out so that you're stiff as a board and can no longer fulfill the exercise requirements on your New Year's resolution list-it will find a way to thwart your good intentions.

That's where Dr. A's Snap Out of It Now! system and breathing techniques come in-to help you tame your self-defeating unconscious, and identify and slay those mental dragons hiding in your dungeon. So simple, yet so life changing. I call my work "the Science of Success"; I think of Dr. A's program as "the Science of Calm." She brings the whole work of transformation into the body. As she's famous for doing with her peak performance clients, Dr. A will help you call forth an unbending serenity and sense of self that can be instantly accessed in life's big moments-in sports, business, or anywhere else. She'll help you take that crucial first step toward opening yourself up so you can attract the good things you need and want into your life.

In short, Dr. A teaches you to snap out of your mental mediocrity. To consciously choose to live your life with vibrations of joy, abundance, love, and wealth so that the Law of Attraction can't help but magnetize abundance right to you.

If you don't know where the "stop button" on your mental treadmill is, or if you're afraid that pushing it will throw you off indefinitely, Snap Out of It Now! will ease your stress and worry. I wish I had known these cutting-edge neurofeedback techniques back when I was a competitive body builder. Or back when my unconscious programming got me into a motorcycle accident that made physical exercise, much less lifting weights, impossible. There are easier ways to learn that we are not our bodies!

I wholeheartedly believe you'll be amazed by the power of this concrete and practical program. You can implement the techniques the minute you read it. No in-depth thinking or trips to the therapist required. You don't even have to believe what she tells you to reap the rewards-just follow her "4 steps to inner joy" and they'll work. The next time you're teetering on the edge of making a positive change in your life, and those familiar mental tapes of I can't do this, I've tried this before, It never works out for me, hold you back from taking that vital last step, you'll know how to snap out of it already! When you see how easily these techniques can change your thinking, you'll become a believer.

Congratulations for attracting this empowering book into your life. And for letting Dr. A take you to your A-game-in sports and in life!

James Arthur Ray
Author of *The Science of Success, Practical Spirituality, and Harmonic Wealth*

Foreword by Tamika Catchings

The title of this book is something we can all relate to. When I first heard about Dr. Adrianne Ahern's book *Snap out of It Now!* and that she wanted me to write the introduction, I was more than honored. I'm not a doctor by any means, and the closest I'll ever come to being one is through my constant access to them through my profession as a professional player in the Women's National Basketball Association and with USA Basketball.

You will love this book because it's applicable to people of all backgrounds and age groups. There are valuable lessons to be learned and information to be absorbed. We've all had ups and downs in our lives, and despite how perfect my life may seem to some, I'm certainly not excluded from having hard times. Even my Olympic gold medal won't deflect the challenges life brings.

By the grace of God, I've made the decision to snap out of it several times in my life: whether it was on the court or in my personal life. By changing certain habits and patterns, I've turned my life around to ensure that my good days outweigh the bad ones. You can do that, too.

During my youth, I never really felt like I fit in with my peers. I was born with a hearing problem that required me to wear bulky hearing aids. I had a speech problem and wore glasses and braces. My classmates made sure that I knew that I was different. I remember running home from school just about every day, wanting to give up and wondering why I had to be so different. The constant negativity that surrounded me in my childhood and the constant tears that flooded my life made me question God's purpose for me on this earth.

In college I truly learned to accept myself and learned that, despite some of the things going on in my life, I needed to take control. I adjusted my attitude and began thinking and being more positive. Reading has always been a passion of mine and my favorite books are those that transform your life and improve your overall well-being. *Snap Out of It Now!* is one of those books. I am very grateful for the positive impact it will make on your life as well.

As you focus on the steps in this book, study each step and apply it to your life. Doing so will help you to grow mentally, physically and spiritually. It took me a long time to accept myself for who I am, and even to this day there are times when the negativity seems to seep in. But, being able to take a step back to refocus helps me to get my mind and life back on target. The breathing techniques and journaling activities that Dr. Ahern teaches can do wonders for all of us.

It is amazing that something as simple as breathing can be used to improve our lives. It is something we all do naturally, yet we often forget how to do it properly. By taking advantage of this book and others like it, we are able to improve our lives and push through our struggles. Reading this book will equip you with the necessary information you need to become the best *you* that you can be. Happiness starts from within, and if we want to get the most out of our lives, it's important that we start with ourselves. By reading this, you are committing yourself to breaking out of a negative mindset and enjoying a happier life.

So come on folks. Snap out of It, take control of your life and don't look back. Challenge yourself to form your own destiny. With the help of this book, you will.

Tamika Catchings
Olympic Gold Medalist, Women's Basketball

Introduction

I developed the Snap Out of It Now! method to put you back in the driver's seat of your life. There is no time for autopilot! This book is an everyperson's guide to do-it-yourself fulfillment, whether fulfillment comes in the form of more self-confidence, more money, more inner focus, more love, or more fun and laughter!

People are looking for the secret to living life fully—to excelling in their chosen field and to experiencing inner joy. Despite pages of affirmations and many hours and dollars worth of therapy, people often find themselves stuck in what they perceive as their own negative destiny.

Snap Out of It Now! demonstrates why the secret continues to elude them—they have been looking in the wrong places, or they just haven't been successful at living their true life paths due to emotional conditioning. Conditioning is a state of mind that is for the most part unconscious. You respond to the expectations and judgments given to you from birth and unknowingly develop emotional roadblocks when you feel unsatisfactory, uncertain or deficient. Without identifying these roadblocks, you have no control over the conditioned thoughts and thus are at their mercy when they are activated. Anger and frustration are often the result, dooming your efforts to failure.

We are all driven to find purpose, joy, money, and happiness in our lives, and to fulfill our birthright. This book is a step-by-step guide to transforming fear, anxiety, self-doubt, anger, and other negative feelings into something completely positive. Eastern secrets to spiritual wellness meet Western psychology to form the perfect personal wellness plan. Unique breathing awareness exercises and psychological worksheets, supported by real case examples from my practice, guide you in releasing yourself from negative thinking and actively succeeding.

My simple therapeutic techniques help you Snap Out of It—your negative conditioning—Now! and find new, simple solutions. My method teaches you to *stop* the negative thinking, *look* at what you really want for yourself, and *listen* to the feelings in your body—your inner guidance—and *breathe* away the negativity. These are the keys to connecting with your inner joy!

Snap Out of It Now! teaches that although we cannot define the mysteries—infinity, the exquisite order of the Universe, and the meaning of life—we can identify negative social conditioning that stops us from seeing the beauty of life and in ourselves. In defining this negative conditioning, we open ourselves up to feeling positive and finding positive solutions for our everyday challenges. In doing so, we are experiencing the mystery of life that surrounds us.

There is an increasing awareness in all of us today that life is passing us by and an emerging desire to be present in the moments of our lives. We are not playing the game of our life fully and with zest, because we spend too much of our life thinking, a process that keeps us in a state of being disconnected from ourselves. We struggle and struggle and struggle to break free from our conditioning—the feelings of depression, anxiety, fear, doubt, guilt, or anger that influence the way we experience ourselves and the circumstances of our lives—and the consequent aggressiveness, passivity, restlessness or impatience with which we then react to the world.

Snap Out of It Now! teaches you to work with your reactions—your resistant negative conditioning—so you will be successful with any project you undertake. You will learn that breathing away negativity and creating inner focus are key to finding your purpose in life quickly, and finally to saying goodbye to the unwanted visitors in your happy homes—feelings of fear, of being overwhelmed, of doubt, anxiety, depression, anger, and unworthiness. You will learn to use awareness of breath to de-condition yourself and experience life more fully!

This book is for those who, when looking into the mirror of their soul, think *I am not living the life I want to be living.* It is for people who are not grasping their innate ability to excel on their true life paths. You now have the key: Snap Out of It Now! opens the door.

With an open heart,

Adrianne Ahern

CHAPTER ONE

We Are Conditioned to Be Unaware

We see only what we *can* see. Each one of us, as human beings, are doing the best we can with what we have—an awareness that has been conditioned by our family, culture, and society. We are *not* aware that we are on *autopilot* as the conditioning has resulted in our pattern of engaging a thought, behavior, and feeling without our conscious awareness.

How do you become the person you were meant to be—strong, self-assured, powerful, and independent? You see these people every day with their million-dollar smiles, radiating confidence with each step they take. You know that inside they feel comfortable, safe, and happy. You imagine that these people share a secret, giving them super-human capabilities to deal with life's emotional roller coasters—otherwise, how could inner joy be so easy?

The truth is, they *do* share a secret, and it's a secret I'll share with you. You are one of those people already—you just don't know it because all the voices you've lived with have told you, *You*

*don't have it! You don't have the right genes! You're not strong
enough! You're not smart enough! Do it my way!* Becoming one of
those people and fulfilling who you were meant to be may seem
impossible, but the real secret to transforming your everyday life
is simple. The first step is realizing that you can leave those voices
behind. Breaking free of that intense negativity with the Snap Out
of It Now! method will change your life forever. You will begin to
hear the little voice that has been whispering to you all these
years, saying, *This is your life! The only requirement is that you live
it your way! You can do it!*

For years, I would go through my life unaware, allowing stress
after stress to snowball until I was one big bundle of bruised
nerves. At the time, I knew that little things shouldn't bog me
down, yet I allowed them to deflate me. A waitress at a diner
would be mean to me; one too many cars in traffic would cut me
off; a dress wouldn't fit right; a bystander would look at me disap-
provingly; and suddenly I would feel that somehow this was all my
fault. I felt judged by people I didn't even know. At the time, I did-
n't even acknowledge my own feelings. I allowed myself to become
overwhelmed and stressed out and accepted this way of life as
normal. The human condition is to suffer, right?

One particularly bad day, my husband said to me, as I am
sure he had said before, "I'm picking up your anxiety." In those
moments, I had not been aware of feeling anxious, and this statement from him provoked feelings of anger in me. Like any trained
psychologist in a defensive mood, my first reaction was to accuse
him of projecting his own anxiety onto me to find a reason for feeling anxious himself. But winning that argument left me feeling
hollow, and my husband unhappy.

In the following few moments, I experienced a powerful awareness. As I acknowledged the feeling of anger within me, I felt my
feelings of anger dissipating and the pressure in my chest soften-
ing. I sat down in silence for a moment, and became aware of subtle sensations of tension and irritability throughout my body. I
thought about everything that had happened over the course of
the day, and realized that I had become more anxious as the day

went on, and was now projecting my feelings of anxiety onto my husband. It was startling for me to realize, with all my education and training, that I had been unaware of feelings—anxiety, fear, jealousy, sadness—within my body, and that these feelings were unconsciously triggering emotional reactions.

For the first time ever, I saw clearly that it wasn't my fault that these little things in my life hadn't gone smoothly, or that I didn't match up to society's ever-changing, impossible standards of perfection. I saw that I didn't have to think like them—you know, the seemingly perfect people. Most importantly, I realized that my feelings of guilt and blame for everything that didn't go well were part of a reality created within my conditioned awareness. I was not to blame. Logically I knew I wasn't, but emotionally I felt I was. I began to see that I could leave the negative and controlling voices of my conditioning behind—I could become my own conditioner.

The feelings of self-doubt and fear began to melt away. As I began to see and acknowledge that my awareness was conditioned, I was able to see how unaware I had been of the control my conditioned thinking had upon my experience of self, others, and the world. The more I became aware of my own thoughts and feelings, the better I felt. After allowing anybody and anything to affect whether I felt good or bad for so long, finally I was in charge of my own mind. My previous view of the misery of being human suddenly went out the window. I was done letting society, culture, and other people control my mind and what I thought of myself. Never had I felt life held so much possibility.

Anybody can make the life change that I did. It isn't a question of whether it is possible to change, or of going to school to become a doctor as I did, or of therapy. It's a matter of when you can commit to opening up your awareness and listening to the voice you have begun to recognize as your own. This voice has always been there, but it is often overwhelmed by the conditioned voices of your environment. It is in the listening to this voice, your true voice, that you become able to distinguish it from those of the conditioning—those of your mother, father, older siblings, teachers, and society. You will become aware that within your conditioned awareness, you have been living your life unaware of the only voice that truly matters: yours. Through your acknowledgment, *I am conditioned to be unaware*, you begin the process of awareness. As soon as you can acknowledge your voice, and how you have been affected by the voices of other people and society as a whole, then positive changes will begin in your life.

If you were walking in the country and a boulder fell on the path before you, you would be able to climb over the boulder or go around it. However, you would first have to acknowledge that it was there. In the same way, people must acknowledge the things that are standing in the way of their self-progress in order to initiate change.

In this chapter, I will assist you in understanding the first steps to acknowledging your voice and overcoming the conditioned mind.

SNAP OUT OF IT NOW! MOMENT

Awareness of Breath

In each Snap Out of It Now! moment, I will introduce an awareness exercise that will help you snap out of the negativity of the conditioned mind. I am going to start by teaching you the key secret behind the Snap Out of It Now! process. It's incredibly simple, but the exercise is critical to your success. It's becoming aware of your breath. Your breath is your key to self-awareness. Your breath is the entry into your body—bringing light to the darkness, warmth to the coldness, and healing to the pain. Your breath is the connector between your mind and body.

Practicing this exercise, and making it a part of your life, will be the single most important thing you can ever do for yourself. If you remember nothing else, remember this—everything starts with the breath. All day long, you have things that require your full attention. In the course of your day—and particularly when you need to focus—*stop, look, listen* and become aware of your breath. Once aware of your breath, you will be focused and present for whatever is in front of you. Breath is the single most important tool to self-realization. As long as you live, breath will never fail you: it is guaranteed.

Become aware of your breath—the breath is the key to being fully present in the moments of your life.

1. Settle into a comfortable position.

2. Close your eyes.

3. Slowly shift attention away from your external surroundings and your thoughts, and focus on your breath.

4. Focus your attention on the breath and become aware of your breathing.

5. Listen to your breathing. Take a generous pause to allow yourself to listen properly. Your breath goes in and out your nose or mouth.

6. Notice that in the moment you are listening. You are not thinking. You are aware, but you're not thinking.

7. When you are ready, gently open your eyes.

With practice, you will experience the power of your breath. Many people spend so much of their time lost in thought; how wonderful to find a tool like listening to your breath that will allow you to be free from thought, even if just for a moment.

WHAT IS HOLDING YOU BACK?

You live seeking happiness and the courage to overcome your fears. Your inner fears and doubts are the voices of your parents, teachers, culture, and the society with which you identified early in childhood. These conditioned fears, doubts and negative thoughts—conditioned identifications—now dictate your behaviors. Conditioned identifications can seem too frightening to face and are therefore repressed by the unconscious mind. Far worse, these fears haunt you, internalized as a dark, unconscious fabrication in the reality of the conditioned mind. Despite what you think or have been told, you don't need therapy, or pills, or hypnosis, or any expensive treatments to overcome this conditioned awareness.

There was a time when I never would have believed that I could own my fears. I simply allowed my conditioned mind—the voices of my past conditioning—to control me. My conditioned voices dictated what I could and could not do. Whether or not I felt good was the result of how I measured up to an intangible standard of perfection set forth by the combination of my parents, a marketing company, television or my set of friends. I was blind to the pain of having these conditioned identifications living in my head and breaking me down. Without knowing why, I felt fear, despair, failure, self-hatred, worthlessness, and selfishness. I thought I had to seek others' support to identify my fears, understand, and overcome them.

Rather than turning within, people tend to turn outwardly. As humans, we have the tendency to turn to myths, fairytales, fantasy, science fiction, and superheroes. They perpetuate the belief that in order to be saved we must either be a superhero or rely on someone or something else. But saved from whom? It is our internal demons that threaten us most. Fueled by these stories, many people seek to emulate their superheroes. This is not inherently negative, but if it is taken too far, this emulation and idolization can create more negative cultural identifications and feelings of defeat. People can no more live up to the impossible standards of fictional superheroes than to society's standards of perfection.

If you're really looking to change your life, you will never find the right story until you uncover your own real life story. And finding your story means uncovering the reality of the conditioning specific to you.

Stop buying into the mythology that we as humans are somehow cursed, forced to carry a heavy emotional weight around like Atlas, balanced only by the human will to survive pain and suffering. This is just another fabrication, designed to allow us to maintain and live with our demons rather than conquer them! You don't have to emulate the superpowers of a god. Beyond the fleeting empowerment of visualizing yourself as more powerful, this will always fall short of helping you to understand the inner workings of your mind and how to change them. You are not meant to be able to separate yourself from emotion, pain, and death. Rather than turning to a new, fairytale conditioning—trying to use one fiction to resolve another—seek to understand your real internal conditioning. Overcome your problems with the mental power of self-awareness that allows you to separate your inner voice from the voices of your conditioning.

You are conditioned to look outside yourself to find the answers to the questions that arise from within. Your journey is to look within yourself.

HOW HAS YOUR "REALITY" BEEN CONDITIONED?

What color are your glasses? Most of you are living your lives without awareness that you are wearing colored glasses. Your reality—what you think, believe, and expect; how you feel; how and what you experience; and how you behave—is created within your conditioned awareness. The process of becoming fully aware of oneself takes time. To open up your awareness of yourself and of the world that surrounds you, ask yourself the following questions:

- What are my thoughts?

- What are my feelings?

- How are my thoughts and feelings influencing my actions in the now?

- Am I aware of the thoughts that enter my consciousness and the feelings that arise within my body?

- Am I aware of how these thoughts and feelings influence and determine the words that come out of my mouth?

- Am I aware of the way I react to people and events?

Imagining the possibilities that heightened awareness could bring you, you struggle with how to enhance your intimacy, caring, compassion, and feeling of connectedness to yourself and others. How do you start to make this happen? Simply acknowledge your conditioned awareness—the color of your glasses—in the moment of intimacy, caring, compassion, and the feeling of being connected to yourself and others. More than just the negatives in your life, your whole way of thinking is repressed in a way that can be unlearned. You can take off your colored glasses and become your own conditioner!

To be truly aware, you must be willing to take action. It might seem like being passive makes for an easier, simpler life, but life only becomes more complex if you rely on others to make decisions for you. Only you can effectively identify and support your personal truths, and thus avoid the frustration that comes from the passive and unrelenting conditioned mind. My favorite poet, Mary Oliver, writes, "And now I understand something so frightening, and wonderful—how the mind clings to the road it knows, rushing through crossroads, sticking like lint to the familiar."

True awareness means making a commitment to break free from your conditioned awareness and begin thinking and feeling for yourself, all the time acknowledging, *I want to be aware.*

In some way, you are aware of your basic relationships—aware of your family and their needs, your friends, coworkers, and others. You are aware of what you are doing, but often you do not think that your actions result from your conditioning.

A client of mine shared that his wife was wrongly accusing him of being too harsh with their daughter about his concerns with her weight. He admitted his concern that she gained 10-15 pounds in her first year of high school. He often asked her, "How are your workouts coming along?" However, his wife and his daughter complained about his "threatening demands" that she lose weight. It wasn't until he acknowledged his own experience as an overweight adolescent that he was able to hear the threatening tone in his voice.

Discovering how you are conditioned is a matter of exploring and acknowledging how you interact with the world and the people in it.

SNAP OUT OF IT NOW! MOMENT

Relationship Analysis

1. Choose one significant relationship in your life—partner, mother, father, child, friend, coworker, or boss—that is troubling you. Get out your journal and find a quiet space where you will not be disturbed. Than, write down:

   - What do you feel is expected of you?

   - What do you expect from this relationship?

   - How do you feel while interacting with this person?

   - What are your basic actions with regard to this relationship?

2. Brainstorm on each action and write down the feelings you have when you do these things.

3. Explore your negative feelings associated with this relationship. Acknowledge their existence, and where they

are in your body. Direct your breath to these areas and imagine these parts of your body breathing. This will increase your self-awareness.

4. Explore your positive feelings associated with this relationship. Acknowledge your positive feelings and notice where they are in your body. Direct your breath to these areas and imagine them breathing. This will increase your awareness of positive feelings and the value you place upon this relationship.

Helpful Hint: When there is a method, there is no madness. Keep an ongoing journal. Pick a notebook that you love, one that makes you happy when you look at it. Pick one of good quality and use it as a tool to get to know yourself better and create your own pathway to success and happiness. Start by writing down feelings and thoughts without trying any specific exercises. Just free-writing is a good start. I will introduce journaling exercises in future chapters. In the beginning, just get used to writing about yourself—what you are feeling and thinking. If you can't think of anything to write about, then write about the last strong emotion you felt, happy or sad.

As you progress, your new awareness will open up your whole perspective on the world in a way you never thought possible. There was a time when my negative conditioning was so bad that I would deny myself the experience and awareness of happiness. I will always remember when I allowed myself to be aware of simple joys in my life, and feel happiness that I didn't initially think I deserved. After making the transition from an unaware life to an aware life, hiking in the mountains or noticing the beauty of wild flowers in springtime became exhilarating. I became aware of my surroundings and aware that I had simply blocked out their beauty by denying my own awareness of it. You will begin to condition yourself to become more and more aware, and a beautiful world will be there—with you in it.

Remember, the challenge is not finding a beautiful world: it is seeing the beauty in the world. Awareness is your first challenge.

CHAPTER TWO

Finding Your Path in Life

Becoming aware of your emotions means becoming aware of your emotional cycle. Self-awareness comes through your acknowledgment and experience of the feelings within your body. When you are within your emotional cycle—*doubt, anger, fear, jealousy, anxiousness, depressiveness*—you are not connected with yourself and you are not aware.

WHO ARE YOU?

You are entitled to be patient with yourself. Regardless of what anyone says, you need to own your problems, but they are not your fault. Understanding yourself and the impact you have on others takes time. And taking your time is not a sin. Time may be fleeting, but you are a worthy cause. Always remember that you are worth the time and effort. Remember this simple truth—the soul doesn't care whether its voice is great or powerful—the soul's purpose is fulfilled by the simple authenticity of expression.

Driven by the desire to understand ourselves and to understand the meaning of life, we are all seekers, including you. Nobody can tell you what your life path should be, but the process of gaining wisdom shares the problem of frustration. We learn and attempt to become truly ourselves, and at the same time we inherit new cultural identifications that come with this expanded knowledge. Importantly, we expand our breadth of knowledge—perhaps surrounding ourselves with new people, places and things, and reflecting on how other people perceive us as we become more perceptive about our own personal behaviors. Improving ourselves, we are rewarded with a sense of accomplishment: we speak better, look better, love better, and play better. We feel good about the positive changes. Suddenly food tastes a little sweeter, and life feels a little smoother. At the same time, new factors enter our lives as we expand and grow, and our lives become more complex. We evaluate ourselves; we dissect ourselves; and we find ways to put ourselves back together again. We react to our experiences, and importantly, continually evaluate ourselves to pinpoint how our cultural identifications have changed. The conscious process of acknowledgement and reaction to our existing identities helps us to identify, and actively assert control over, our personal growth and life path.

As a psychologist, I notice that many people confuse this cycle of understanding—taking in new information and processing how it has affected you—with starting all over again, which is depressing and discouraging. In fact, rather than a static, circular pattern, we can create an upward, spiral pattern of change in our lives.

Changing your city, job, or relationship does not equate to a re-creation of who you are. Outward changes merely open you up to the possibility of empowering yourself. Changing your physical location has little to do with altering your self-knowledge, although it does create opportunities for life-altering experiences. Mental location has everything to do with altering the way we experience life and our selves.

Each time you undergo or initiate a life change, take a deep breath and realize that your identity is already formed. You are the person you were meant to be, and from now on things will only get better. Each change is something one reacts to, but you are never alone or without a self. There is no need to recreate yourself, only to open yourself up to awareness and understanding. Remember that each time you acknowledge your reactions to how you cope with the process of growing, learning, and seeking, you are coming closer to having inner peace and orienting your life path positively. In other words, as you acknowledge your reaction of impatience with self-growth, your awareness is brought into the present moment and you are reconnected with the experience of self. However, when you do not acknowledge your reaction, then your conditioned awareness is reinforced, you are disconnected from yourself, and you remain feeling impatient.

FINDING YOUR PATH IN LIFE: THE CYCLE OF UNDERSTANDING

Most of us are conditioned to believe that we can think our way out of experiencing difficult feelings that arise within. Whenever we experience anger toward someone, rather than allow ourselves the natural experience of feeling anger (which in itself would be an acknowledgment of ourselves), we move quickly from the physically stressful feeling of anger to the cognitive experience of thinking about how to resolve this feeling of anger. We are conditioned to think we can resolve our experience of anger, fear, or jealousy, and therefore we distance ourselves from the uncomfortable experience of these feelings by attempting to figure it out cognitively. We rationalize justifications for being angry, and then make sense of the anger by thinking about anger resolution. The quick fix of rationalization, however, does not prevent the next outburst of anger—or resolve the initial incidence.

Angry feelings will find a nesting place within the body, and then the thinking mind denies and suppresses the feeling. Without acknowledgement and experience of the feelings, the anger will remain, reinforcing your conditioned awareness as well as creating physical disturbances within your body. As you allow yourself to acknowledge and experience anger, notice and stay with the feeling, keeping your attention focused on the emotional sensation. You will notice that the anger slowly dissipates, and the need to mentally resolve the anger disappears.

The thinking mind attempts to resolve feelings through problem-solving, but when logic fails the mind rejects, denies, and then blames someone else for the feelings that continue to exist. Identifying, acknowledging and experiencing negative emotions as part of your emotional cycle will help you to work through the traumas and negative emotions you experience. In this book, you will learn to avoid being caught up in solving problems. You will acknowledge and experience the feeling of anger, sense the feeling dissipate, and then open to the experience of yourself—no longer angry—in the moment.

A person can quote catchphrases automatically, without actually knowing what the words mean. This is a conditioned reaction. Without awareness, one might say, "I love you," "I don't want to hurt you," "I am sorry," or "Trust me." We listen as we have been conditioned to listen and what we hear is being heard through the screen of our conditioned awareness.

Do you think before you speak? Do you *stop, look,* and *listen* to your emotions and to how you want to express what you feel through speech? If you are unaware of the impact of your choice of words, you may be using words to navigate through people on your life path, rather than connecting people into your life path. If you feel disconnected or alienated from others, it could be that words are getting in the way of your attempts to communicate and thus hindering your relationships. Many of us are conditioned not to be aware of our feelings, rendering our emotionally indicative words impotent as tools for communication.

Feeling unsure of where you fit in on the scale from connected to disconnected through language? Think about how many times a day you use a phrase that indicates an emotion you feel, and compare that number to the number of times you use that same phrase without indicating an emotion you feel. If you will not remember your count, bring a notepad with you for one day to tally certain phrases. Mentally or physically note how many times you say, "I love you;" "I'm sorry;" and any other popular phrase. You might be saying, "I love you" as an alternative to "good-bye," or "I am sorry," to move a conversation along, or to end an argument.

Misusing emotional phrases when you do not feel emotionally about what you are saying causes three noticeable problems. First, you desensitize other people to the emotional power of these phrases, and the words no longer have the same power when you want to use them to express your feelings honestly. Second, you create discord and disconnection with other people by creating misunderstandings or failing to correct disagreements. Third, you bottle up emotions inside yourself, creating a bomb of discontent waiting to explode. The simplest way to deal with these problems is to recognize the phrases you have been conditioned to use automatically. *Stop, look,* and *listen* each time you use these phrases to bring awareness to this conditioning. Soon, you'll find yourself creating new ways to express yourself. Always remember that the use of an automatic phrase is a conditioned reaction, and can be unlearned.

Emily,[1] who had just lost a parent, shared with me the feelings of confusion that were coupled with various bodily disturbances—the muscles in her neck and lower back were producing pain. When asked by friends and family how she was feeling, she would simply say she was sorry, and close down emotionally. During childhood, Emily explained, "I was never allowed to be angry, and I don't know how to recognize it when I am experiencing it." Like many children, if she did become angry, she would be forced to apologize for her outburst. As an adult, she simply skipped the step of recognizing her anger or acting angrily, and would lifelessly admit blame and apologize.

Like Emily, many of us are not encouraged to express negative feelings and as such have been conditioned to suppress or deny feelings of anger, jealousy, sadness, or grief. When suppressed or denied, these feelings—expressed as sensations in the body such as tightness in the chest, stomach upset, headache—can become

---

1. Names have been changed to respect the privacy of individuals.

isolated and run their own program which sets up the disturbance.

There are some of you who are conditioned not to be aware of and express positive feelings like happiness, joy, and love. When they arise within you, you may not be aware of what it is you are feeling, and you might not know how you would go about expressing what you are feeling. As you recognize and experience both your positive and negative emotions, you will enhance your sensitivity, understanding, and intuition—about yourself and about how other people feel. Becoming aware of self through awareness of your full range of feelings—your inner guidance—is a central feature of the Snap Out of It Now! method and the key to self-awareness!

Moving beyond this emotional and linguistic level of conditioned awareness is an ongoing practice.

SNAP OUT OF IT NOW! MOMENT

Awareness of Feeling

When you are unable to express a feeling—anger or love—acknowledge that you are conditioned to be unaware of the feelings that arise within you and that you are unaware of how to express these feelings. Becoming aware of one's own feelings is a huge emotional step.

Here, I ask you simply to take a break from your day:

1.   Settle into a comfortable chair and sit with your back straight—not stiff—and use a pillow to support your lower back with feet flat on the floor. Sit tall with your chin slightly tucked in. Or lie down, if sitting is uncomfortable.

---

2.   Relax your jaw and allow your tongue to touch the roof of your mouth gently. Relax your belly. Now, bring awareness to your breathing.

3.   Feel your breath going in and out through your nose or mouth. Focus on your breath; this will allow the internal chatter to slow down or stop.

4.   *Stop*, *look*, and *listen* to what you are feeling right now. This may take practice.

5.   Sense, acknowledge and experience the feelings within you.

6.   Breathe (direct your breath) to the feeling sensation in your body, wherever it may be.

7.   You are becoming aware of feelings within you.

Awareness comes from being with your senses—taste, smell, sound, touch, and sight. In any one moment of your day, practice breathing in the awareness of your surroundings.

CHAPTER THREE

The Touchstone of Incongruity

As human beings we *know* we can do better—we believe we are capable of living the life we dream for ourselves. The soul speaks to us in the language of *feeling sensations. Incongruity* is a feeling sensation, which may manifest as doubt and uncertainty, and this sensation provokes us in our thinking that there is another way—*our way.*

WHAT DOES INCONGRUITY MEAN TO YOU?

We have all felt moments where something felt off, but we couldn't quite pinpoint what. We have all had the feeling that somehow life is not what it ought to be, but ignored it. We have all thought about this feeling of discord fleetingly, but then we move on to living our life. This feeling of discord is what I call *incongruity.* The awareness of our incongruity is awareness of the difference between who we are and who we have been conditioned to be.

You don't have to live with feelings of incongruity. Your conditioned identity is the sum of your *conditioned identifications—* thoughts that have become more powerful through your identification with them. These include all of the negative thoughts, stories, judgments, expectations, and beliefs that have become truths within your conditioned awareness. The conditioned identifications in your mind trap your true self behind a wall of limitations and expectations of what you should be. All people are conditioned, and are conditioned to travel their conditioned path. Many people live their lives without conscious awareness that their thoughts—the voices of our fathers, mothers, older siblings, teachers, coaches, and friends—impact and interfere with their ability to discover who they truly are. To break down the walls of your conditioning and stop repressing who you are, you must become aware of what is standing in your way.

Incongruity is a touchstone. It indicates that you have entered into the awareness—however subtle—that your identity is conditioned. The feeling of incongruity alerts you to the recognition that something is amiss. The level of awareness in each person varies, and therefore the awareness of the feeling of incongruity may arise early in life for some, later in life for others, and may be present throughout life if never addressed.

IT'S A STRUGGLE TO FIND YOURSELF, BUT YOU CAN DO IT!

Start expecting more out of life. You can become more than your conditioning, and have everything you ever wanted—but in order to initiate change you must first acknowledge the affect your conditioning has over your identity and actions. Conditioning is a state of mind: you respond to the expectations and judgments given to you from birth, and unknowingly develop emotional roadblocks when you feel unsatisfactory, uncertain or deficient. Without identifying these roadblocks—the incongruity within— you have no control over the conditioned thoughts and thus are at their mercy when they are activated.

As a child, Ben listened a lot and spoke very little. He always had a desire to communicate, but with three older brothers, he could never speak quickly enough or loudly enough. He remembered feeling deeply about things that happened in the family and feeling the desire to share, but his attempts at communicating were met with failure more often than not. He developed feelings of tension and anxiety surrounding his attempts to speak. When he did speak, he learned to emulate the voices of his mother, father or brothers, and he never really felt understood. As he grew older, he became skilled at saying only what he had been conditioned to say.

Ben learned not to verbalize his internal thoughts and feelings because he felt they weren't worthy of expression. He had a sense of incongruity between the desire to speak, be heard, and understood, and the fear that he couldn't speak, be heard, or understood. As an adult, he consciously attempted to avoid circumstances in which he would be asked to speak or write, but he was required to do so in his business life. Ben developed a stress disorder, and this was his wake-up call to change his life.

When Ben came to see me, he only knew that something was out of balance. First we worked on self-awareness, because he needed to come to terms with the conditioning that his thoughts weren't worthy of voicing. Once we identified the problem—that Ben was living unconsciously within his conditioned awareness— he began to acknowledge the voices in his head, such as *No one is interested in your thoughts or feelings,* as the voices of his past conditioning. Ben discovered that it is in the acknowledgment and acceptance of self that the perception of worthiness is born. Soon, he was able to see that he could learn and condition himself to speak with confidence and grace.

From there, he could begin to allow his identity to surface and learn how to communicate more effectively, both with himself and others. He needed to make a commitment to allowing himself the liberty of growing as an individual and breaking away from what he had been conditioned to do and say. He began to use the exercises he had learned in multiple situations. After all, awareness is just the first step. The situations we face in life are many, and we must continually acknowledge the incongruity we feel, acknowledge and accept ourselves as living within a conditioned awareness, identify the conditioning, and break through to allow our inner selves to grow.

What we do with the awareness of the incongruity makes the difference between moving forward with conscious awareness of ourselves and allowing our perception of others to box us into negative situations where we become half-heartedly what we think others want us to be.

When I sense incongruity in my life, I listen to my inner voice and proceed cautiously, first attempting to understand myself and what might be holding me back, which then allows me to move forward confidently to make the life decision that is best for me.

There is a point where you are presented with the choice of either facing and acknowledging your conditioning, or taking the seemingly easier path of ignoring the feeling that something isn't right, denying the importance of the incongruence, and falling back on the deceptive comfort of your conditioning. However frightening it is to face the incongruity you experience, in the long run the things you can do to escape or avoid awareness will take longer and be harder for you.

Instead of rationalizing why something that feels wrong should be right according to the advice of others, allow yourself to feel the incongruity in your life and your innate desire for positive change. You may have the urge to avoid feelings of incongruity because you believe that you will have to change the way in which you are approaching and living your life—your traditional script. Truthfully, pretending to be happy to avoid an incongruity is a much scarier and less rewarding emotional journey. Eventually the false happiness fades away, and again you will feel discontent when you have more discord in your life. In fact, the feeling of discord will never be lost until the incongruity is resolved.

You don't have to make the mistakes that my clients have in the past. If you acknowledge the incongruity you feel, you can become aware of your conditioning and see it for what it really is—a stumbling block to resolving the unease. At this point of realization and awareness, you will have the opportunity to make changes in your life.

RESOLVING INCONGRUITY

So let's talk about you. I hear things like, "I want to find my voice," and "I want to fully express myself" a lot from my patients. What does this really mean? Why do we feel such distaste when we observe and confront who we are? Why do we suddenly fall back into the conditioned identity of ourselves?

The fact is that our conditioned identifications are a part of us, and have their roots in our earliest experiences. If you overlook your past—any uncomfortable facets of reality and your conditioning—then you might be able to see the person who you want to become, but you will not be able to see *how* to become that person. The following is a model for what to do to transcend incongruity instead of just dreaming about the future.

YOUR PATHWAY TO SUCCESS—THE STEPS TO MOVING BEYOND INCONGRUITY

Embrace Awareness of Incongruity

First, you must become aware of when you are feeling incongruous. Remember, incongruity arises when a conditioned identification provokes an inner experience of conflict and uncertainty. It arises when you come face to face with those aspects of your conditioned identity that feel "wrong" because you are internally at odds with something you have been conditioned to think, believe, say or do.

- When you feel incongruous, it may be experienced as anger toward who you are—your conditioned identity—as you believe the conditioning does not reflect the person you feel you really are or really want to be. You may have the thought, *I am not living the life I should or could be living,* or simply feel dissatisfied. This is a valid thought—don't ignore it!

- You may also experience incongruity as the vague feeling that a mistake has been made, accompanied by a negative physical response such as a headache, stress, hives, or a stomach ache, or perhaps just a feeling of being off balance. It is important to pay attention to your physical as well as your mental responses. Your health can be a good indicator of what is going on inside your head.

Identify the Problem

Second, don't be afraid to admit that you have a problem. Incongruity is a wake-up call often disguised as a problem.

Unfortunately, awareness often stops at the initial alert to the incongruity. Instead of becoming aware of the incongruity, people often turn their focus toward trying to eliminate the feeling of incongruity, by ignoring or repressing it beneath conditioned beliefs. Why? The feeling of incongruity is scary because it seems to indicate that they will need to change something about their conditioning and their lifestyle.

Only you can decide:

- Am I happy and content with life as it is?

or:

- Do I want to be free to create the life I deserve—filled with joy, love, and abundance?

Within the hold of your traditional script and your conditioned identity, your conditioning continues to tell you what you should think, do, want, and believe in attempts to resolve the incongruity. However, resolution cannot take place within the conditioning. Like Ben, despite our love for other people in our lives, there are times where we need to put ourselves first and realize that we need to spend time and attention on ourselves—and focus on what we want, not what other people want from us. Your inner thoughts, desires, goals and feelings are valid: they represent your true self. It is your birthright to express them, even if others may not agree with you.

SNAP OUT OF IT NOW! MOMENT

Identifying Incongruity

Here is an exercise that will help you to identify the negative conditioning that is creating incongruity in your life. Make sure to have your journal handy.

The next time you feel an incongruity:

1. *Stop* and acknowledge the feeling of incongruity.

2. *Look* at what is happening within you. Where does the feeling arise in the body—head, neck, tummy, chest? What is the sensation—tightness, tension, aches, fussiness, tingling? Describe where it is and what it feels like.

3. *Listen* to the feeling of incongruity. What is it signaling? From where might it be stemming? What thoughts are presents? What thoughts arise? Write these thoughts down.

4. *Breathe* to the feeling of incongruity within your body wherever it may be.

5. Journal your experience. Spend as much time as you would like with your journal and let yourself engage the process of writing down whatever enters your consciousness. Do not edit—if not editing is a challenge for you, put the journal away. You can go back and read it later, when the desire to edit is no longer so strong.

Focus on You!

Third, allow yourself the time to center yourself. The creativity of the music we like, whether it's classical, rock, country, pop or jazz, is palpable to us. Do we not listen to the music we love and feel a kind of peace within? I read, write, and recite poetry, which opens my mind to creativity and allows me to access the deeper part of myself. We are often drawn to art, or to creating art, to express something that we are feeling in our everyday lives but perhaps cannot express. When we find artistic expression that we relate to on a fundamental level, we are experiencing congruity with the world we live in. It's important to allow yourself the time to do things that help you feel inner peace and congruity in your life. When you make time for yourself, then you will be making time to address your needs in life and start becoming who you want to be, instead of just thinking about the regrets you have about who you wish you were.

SNAP OUT OF IT NOW! MOMENT

Break Time

Take 30 minutes a day to be alone and do something you enjoy. Don't use your phone, TV, computer, or PDA. In a fast-paced world, it's hard to give yourself a break, so do yourself a favor and schedule a minimum of 30 minutes of "me" time everyday, doing something that makes you feel good— whether that's listening to music, reading or writing poetry, journaling, walking, meditating, or something else that allows you to stay connected with yourself. A good way to feel better about yourself is to treat yourself with the same love and respect that you give to other people—rewards included!

RECOGNIZE OTHERS MAY DISAGREE

Fourth, if you choose to work with the incongruity, you must be willing to face yourself with awareness and honesty. Others may disagree with the changes you are making in your life. Once you make the commitment to begin confronting your conditioning, you will start to feel a sense of exhilaration and enthusiasm that you have finally stumbled onto the right track. Caution! You must also recognize that it will not always be easy, as it is within the conditioning that you have learned to feel loved and accepted. Once you begin to break free from the conditioning, others may react negatively as the real you provokes feelings of confusion, rejection, jealousy or fear in them.

At this point you will have a choice—either continue the confrontation with your conditioned identity, or return to your conditioned awareness where you know you will be provided with repeated moments of relief; moments where you feel loved and not rejected. Just as I was too frightened to go against my conditioning by saying no to my first marriage proposal, people are usually more afraid of doing something their family and friends won't approve of than doing something they themselves don't approve of. In the short run, the path of least resistance may be easier, but in the end, don't forget that you must always live with yourself. If you make decisions you can't live with just to please others, you're delaying the sense of freedom that comes with acknowledging your conditioned awareness and breaking down the walls of your conditioning.

SNAP OUT OF IT NOW! MOMENT

Ways to Say No to the Conditioned Voices

When you begin the transition from living unconsciously within your conditioned identity to becoming your own conditioner, you will find it helpful to have some tools you can access freely and immediately. I have included some examples of what you can choose to say or how you can choose to respond in those situations when you perceive other people—your boss, parent, lover, friend, or even a stranger—wanting you to conform to their idea of what is best for you.

1. Say *no*. Do not give any reasons or make excuses—this only gives the other person more information to work with in their effort to convince you to say *yes*.

2. When feeling unsure or uncomfortable as to how to respond to your boss or business associate, take a calming breath and say, "I'd like to give that some thought."

3. If saying no is too uncomfortable or you feel it is not acceptable—say *maybe*. This will buy some time and take away the pressure to respond immediately.

4. Say nothing. I tell my clients to say nothing in situations where they feel unable to say no and where saying yes would feel wrong. Silence can be golden: you can't be quoted! Take a conscious breath and simply don't say anything. Stay connected with your sense of honesty, self-worth, and integrity. We so often feel a response is required when it isn't. Saying nothing

may allow you to remain congruent with your inner sense of self.

5. If you feel compelled to explain yourself, then first take a conscious breath and silently think about how you honestly feel. Breathe with your sense of honesty, self-worth, and integrity. Feeling connected with yourself, go ahead and state your opinion aloud.

6. Take a moment to think. If the impulse is strong to say yes when you want to say no, then breathe to the feeling of this impulse within your body. Using breath in this way will allow the impulse to dissipate and leave you with the ability to consciously choose the most congruent answer.

Commit to Your Self-Awareness Plan—Create a Focused Intention for Yourself

Fifth, make a plan. We make commitments all the time—to stop being so angry, to stop eating so unhealthy, to work harder, be more understanding, and to be more compassionate and loving. But we cannot truly commit to improving ourselves as individuals without first committing to opening our awareness and acknowledging our conditioned identity.

SNAP OUT OF IT NOW! MOMENT

Visualizing Success

When you feel an incongruity, then this feeling will point you to the facet of yourself that needs attention. Snap out of thinking about how you want to live, and go directly to living your life the way you want.

1. Begin by creating an intention for yourself—an inner picture of what you want to manifest for yourself. Maybe this picture is of you as a loving, understanding, and compassionate spouse and parent, as a golfer on the PGA Tour, or as a financially successful businessperson.

2. When you have a clear inner picture of what you intend to create for yourself, notice the feeling within your body that accompanies this inner picture: joy, appreciation, and enthusiasm.

3. Make a commitment to focus on this intention, and on the inner image and feeling you have identified. By visualizing your goal, you are conditioning yourself—body, mind, and spirit—to manifest your intention. Return to this visualization several times throughout your day. You are becoming your own conditioner!

Stick with It

Sixth, change doesn't happen overnight. Change is an ongoing process. Be patient with yourself, but stay true to your focused intention for yourself. As you open your eyes in the morning, and just as you lay your head on the pillow at night, say your intention out loud. In the moments of your day—every time you catch yourself engaging negative self-talk or criticism of others—*stop* and acknowledge your conditioned judgment of self and others, *look* at the inner image you intend for yourself, and *listen* to the feeling of joy, appreciation, and enthusiasm within your body that accompanies your focused intention. *Breathe* with the feelings within your body.

To close this chapter, I want to leave you with one last Snap Out of It Now! exercise that will help you to focus on your breath and more easily resolve incongruity as it arises.

Breathing Awareness Meditation: The Touchstone of Incongruity

Awakening to incongruity is the threshold to becoming consciously aware of yourself and to becoming your own conditioner. The following exercise is to be engaged in those moments of incongruity. It will support you in your discovery of who you are and in finding your way.

1.   Sitting right where you are, settle into a comfortable position and close your eyes.

2.   Become aware of your breath. Feel it going in and out through your nose and mouth.

3.   Allow yourself to become fully aware of the internal discord—incongruity. As you bring this experience to your awareness, ask yourself:

   •   What are you thinking?

   •   What is the feeling present within your body?

   •   Allow your attention to stay as long as you can with the feeling.

4.   Breathe to this feeling in your body wherever it may be. It might be very subtle.

5. Breathe in toward the physical feeling. Focus your breath and imagine it going to the physical location of this feeling. As you breathe this way, you are acknowledging the incongruity within and connecting with yourself: body, mind, and spirit.

6. Exhale slowly and as you exhale feel your body releasing the feelings of discord within.

7. When you feel ready, gently open your eyes.

CHAPTER FOUR

Conditioning—The Identity-Determining Process

We are all being conditioned—programmed, trained, persuaded, convinced, taught, and even seduced—all the time, even from before our birth. We believe we know who we are and we believe we can change our reality. We are not aware that we are living within a *conditioned reality.*

WHAT IS CONDITIONING?

Direct conditioning, the onset of conditioning that usually comes from our mother or core conditioner, begins as the fetus develops in the womb. When we're in the womb, our mother's conditioning is being fed to us. At the same time, our genes, which come from our mother and our father and all our ancestors, are conditioning us as well. These genes are conditioning us physically, intellectually, psychologically, emotionally, and spiritually.

If you could remember yourself as an embryo developing in the womb, then you could feel your eyes becoming blue. You could possibly feel the shape of your head forming, and the features of your face shifting and developing in a certain way. Were you able to remember your physical being's formation, you would be remembering the initiation of the conditioning process at the biochemical level.

At birth, we enter into the environmental conditioning of our mother and father and our families, who have been and are being conditioned by our culture, religion, and society. The environmental conditioning will affect the manner in which your mind and your body lay down biochemical patterns, and those patterns, which are conditioned by our genes, will affect the conditioning that we will be exposed to in our environment. Thus begins a feedback loop within the conditioning process affecting who we are.

Imagine that you have just been born and you can feel the biochemical patterns within yourself. You begin to hear sounds, you begin to receive smells, you begin to sense changes of light and perceptions of color, and you feel sensations of touch. The environment begins to send its signals to you, and you begin to react to these signals. In this reaction, you experience the initial conditioning effects of the environment. At the moment you experience your mother, your core conditioner, looking into your face and holding you for the first time, the conditioning process between the two of you begins. The expression on her face conditions you, and the sounds you utter condition her in return. The manner in which she touches you conditions you and the way you feel to her conditions her. How you smell and taste to one another will also affect the way the conditioning process continues.

You respond to the core conditioner with the relaxation of your little body. Can you imagine how your response will condition her, and then in turn her response will continue conditioning you? Imagine what your little body might feel without such conditioning: without touch, without soothing sounds, without warmth from another, or without human presence. We need to be conditioned or we will die. If flung out of the nest like a bird, we will not automatically take flight. We will not survive.

There have been instances of human babies discovered who were raised by wolves and who survived. In the absence of a human conditioning—language, interaction, location, way of life—

the children found it difficult to assimilate into the unfamiliar human environment. Babies who have no conditioning—no warmth or love from man or beast—get sick and die. Conditioning is necessary for survival, as it is responsible for teaching us to protect ourselves from harm, to participate competently in the world, to master our intellectual and physical abilities, and to achieve great things in our lives.

In our environment, we are conditioned to many things. We are conditioned to like some things and to dislike others, to use and pronounce words in a certain way, and to judge some things as good and others as bad. Everything is conditioned—from the manner in which we interact with our environment, to how we think about ourselves, to how we think about others. The specific things to which we are conditioned are more important to us, and begin to take on a reality that becomes specific to us: our conditioned reality.

We enter the world with our genetically-determined innate abilities and proclivities—our temperament, if you will—and then interact with and are conditioned by our environment, including our parents, friends, schools, church, government, and so forth. Each person has a truly unique temperament. Our temperaments affect how we interact with our environment, and thus how we are conditioned.

Let's try something. Imagine you go into a room and a dog jumps toward you and starts to lick you. How will you greet the dog? Your reaction—feelings and actions—will be different than, say, a friend's reaction. You might fall to the floor with excitement to wrestle with the dog, allowing the dog to lick you all over. Or, you might stiffen defensively, feel emotionally detached from the animal, and react rigidly to the dog's advances. These differences reflect differences in temperament as well as differences in how we have been conditioned with regard to familiarity with dogs. Your interaction is indicative of your conditioning. Simple? Yes. To recognize it? Not necessarily.

We are conditioned to react in a particular way in almost every imaginable situation, and most often we do not take the time to

41

> To identify with a thought is to become the same as that thought. For example, when you identify with a thought *I don't have any talents* or *I'm not smart enough,* you believe this thought and see it as representing the truth of who you are. Therefore, until you bring the thought to your awareness, you are unable to separate the thought from your perception of yourself.

stop and become aware of how and why we are reacting. Actually, many people are not even aware that they are indeed reacting. If I ask you, "Why do you react so aggressively to someone who takes your place in the grocery line?" You might just say, "Well, doesn't everyone react that way?" No, everyone doesn't react the way you do. Some people are conditioned to react with compassion, passive acceptance, or even self-blame. Until we bring awareness to our conditioning, it will continue to determine who we are and how we react to ourselves, others, and to our life circumstances!

So, what do I mean by *the conditioning?*

Conditioning is a state of mind—a belief system—that is unconscious. The content of this belief system is our interpretation of the voices of our earliest childhood—mother, father, siblings, teachers, friends and society—with which we have become identified. We don't question from where these voices originated, because we don't think of them as separate from ourselves. They appear to be our emerging voice. I refer to these conditioned voices—inner thoughts, expectations, judgments, and beliefs—as *conditioned identifications*. The sum of these conditioned identifications becomes the reality in which we live: our *conditioned reality*.

As we move through childhood, conditioning distances us from our true voices. As adults, we are unaware of the conditioning, and we live our lives disconnected from our true voices. We live our lives thinking and reacting according to this conditioned belief system. In this way, we are destined—or doomed—to live according to this conditioned reality.

Some authors refer to the conditioning as the *egoic self* or *false* self. Film-makers have referred to the conditioning as being within a computer-like program in which we are playing, or acting out, a preassigned role. Still others refer to the state of conditioning as the colored glasses we were born wearing. I will often use the term *sleepwalking,* as it clearly illustrates how we need to wake up to ourselves—awaken from our conditioned reality—and take charge of our own lives.

Within the chapters of this book, you will confront your belief system. You will learn, and have the opportunity, to bring these conditioned voices to your conscious awareness, where they no longer have the power to impact and interfere with how you live life.

SNAP OUT OF IT NOW! MOMENT

Follow Your Breath: Follow Your Feeling

The following breathing awareness exercise will allow you to check in with yourself. How are you experiencing the information you are taking in? This is a wake-up call! Acknowledging that you are living unaware within a conditioned reality is a huge step in self-awareness. Be compassionate, nurturing, and patient with yourself.

1. Sitting right where you are, settle into a comfortable position and close your eyes.

2. Become aware of your breath. Listen to it as it goes in and out through your nose and mouth.

3. Follow your breath with your attention as it travels in through your nose and enters your body.

4. What is the feeling you are experiencing right now within your body?

5. Allow yourself to acknowledge and experience the feeling you are having right now.

The way to identify your authentic voice is through the process of connecting with your true self, by acknowledging and experiencing the feelings within your body. Use your breath as a tool to help your mind and body connect. In this chapter on conditioning, you are learning to recognize your conditioning, and how the conditioned voices in your head affect the way you think, make decisions, act and react. Once you master my simple self-awareness techniques, then you will be capable of changing—de-conditioning—the reactions that are affecting you negatively. But let's take things one step at a time. Later in the book, I will explain in detail how to confront, identify, and de-condition negative reactions. For now, just remember that *why* you are who you are is not as important as truly seeing and acknowledging *who* you are. This chapter is about understanding who you are as a conditioned person. From here, you will learn to take control of the conditioning, become your own conditioner, and be the person you were meant to be.

FACING OUR CONDITIONING

Truthfully, most of us really don't want to face our conditioning. We don't want to see who we really are. My premise is that we must wake up and face who we are—our conditioning—before we can fully become who we are meant to be. Though we must treat our negative conditioning as if it is a part of us, our essential selves do lie beneath our conditioning. We often try to change the parts of ourselves that we don't like, hoping this will heal us and allow us to be the person we want to be. We try to develop new behaviors, to stop old behaviors, to live a different lifestyle, to take on a new perspective, or to achieve our goals. However, we often fail to address the conditioning that has created who we already are. This makes progress from our current state almost impossible.

Instead of focusing within ourselves, we focus on problems as they arise in life. *Why did this happen to me? How did this happen? Who is at fault? When did something go wrong? Where was a mistake made?* We think that if we will get to the bottom of the problem, there will be one single thing we can change that will resolve everything. Then we are perplexed, appalled, and anguished to find ourselves repeating the same behaviors, and continuing to have the same problems in our lives.

Some people say that if we are not aware of the past we will repeat it. I say that unless you are aware of your conditioning then you will be doomed to repeat your past mistakes. Even when we are aware of the past, we repeat our mistakes. Only when we become aware of the conditioning and make a commitment to change are we able to change the future. Understanding the origins of our problems is never enough. Understanding a problem is beneficial as long as we understand that problem through the lens of ourselves. To clarify, we must understand the way our conditioning plays a part in our negative emotional reactions. Knowing the answers to questions such as, *Why am I the way I am"* and *What happened?* does not help us to change. Even if we understand the answers to these questions, that will not stop us from continuing to react in the same negative ways, over and over again. If we are only quantifying and qualifying our conditioners, then we are simply playing the blame game. We must face our conditioning in order to be capable of moving beyond the conditioning. The way out is the way in.

Other people make mistakes and do things that are hurtful to us or affect us negatively. But you can't change other people; you can only change yourself and your behaviors. In later chapters, you will be given exercises that will allow you to confront and identify your specific conditioning. For now, don't become overwhelmed by trying to unravel your conditioning and figure out exactly who or what is responsible. Instead, just start by recognizing and acknowledging that you have been conditioned.

SNAP OUT OF IT NOW! MOMENT

Starting to Recognize Your Conditioning

To begin this recognition:

1. Look at how you live.

2. Notice how you feel about yourself.

3. Become aware of your self-talk. Is it predominantly negative?

4. Observe the manner in which you think about others.

5. Witness the way you react to your self-talk, other people, and events.

You may want to use your journal to write about your observations, or you may want to just allow yourself to experience this process. You will have ample opportunities to journal in later chapters. Do what feels most congruent within yourself.

When I was a little girl, my family enjoyed debating and arguing—sometimes yelling—at the dinner table, often using an encyclopedia to resolve the dinner-table drama. Meanwhile I would clam up, feeling small and inadequate. The noise of their loud

voices frightened me and the quickness of their responses inti-
mated me, and I did not know how to contribute in these discussions. My chest would tighten, and my mind would go blank.
Later I would beat myself up over it, asking myself, *Why can't I
think of a way to contribute?* or *How can they be so sure of themselves—someone has to be wrong?* I could spend as long as I
wanted trying to dissect my flaws, trying to figure out the reasons
why and exactly how I was conditioned, trying to blame my family
for behaving the way they do, or trying to change my family
dynamic, but in the end, none of that would be productive.

Later in life, I realized that many families become similarly
heated during discussions, and while I might perceive that it isn't
necessarily the best way to communicate, I certainly couldn't
change my family dynamic, never mind anyone else's. Instead, I
learned to accept that I was conditioned to react by clamming up,
to be fearful of and protect myself from loud, aggressive conversa-
tions. While I could not change their method of communication—
and still cannot, I could change my own reaction, learn to relax,
feel more at ease despite the drama surrounding me, allow myself
to validate my own opinions by voicing them without allowing fear
to inhibit me from being a part of the group.

I simply needed to know who I was: I was a person who felt
afraid of a voicing her thoughts and feelings in the midst of a
whole bunch of other people's loudly expressed opinions. I realized I needed to overcome that fear in order to participate in my
family dynamic. In my career, I have since learned Cognitive
Behavioral Therapy, Psycho-Dynamic Therapy, and Rational-
Emotive Therapy, and helped countless patients achieve their
personal goals, but still none of this will ever give me the power to
change my family and the way they communicate. Knowing and
accepting who I was and then learning to work with my conditioned reactions proved more important than asking why.

Recognizing Conditioning in Day-to-Day Life

All of the behaviors we choose to engage in our everyday lives are conditioned, and we, if we give them any thought, will recognize some of them as conditioned behaviors. The conditioning we are referring to here is that which is within the grasp of our conscious awareness. We know our parents conditioned us to brush our teeth, eat breakfast, and go to school; we know our teachers conditioned us to read and write, and do our homework; we know our social groups are conditioning us as to how to interact with each other, wear the right clothes, and to share the same language; and we know society is conditioning us to behave acceptably, so that we exercise self-control in our speech and in our actions.

Often in families, different generations have different ideas of what is or is not acceptable behavior. My mother has been conditioned to think that large families are natural and good. Her daughter-in-law, in speaking of a couple she knows who have eleven children, laughingly refers to that situation as obscene. Whenever this subject is brought up, the result is animosity between my mother and my sister-in-law because of the differences in their conditioning. It's easy to see how the way one is conditioned—what one believes as the truth—can so easily create conflict in a relationship.

We talk about the effects of advertising in magazines and on television, and if we think about it, we may be aware that when we wear a particular type of clothing or act a certain way that these behaviors have been conditioned by what we have observed in the media. We know we are being conditioned, but we do not acknowledge the conditioning. We don't say to ourselves, *I'm conditioned. I buy Mac lipstick because I am conditioned to believe it is the best, and I'm conditioned to believe I will be perceived more favorably while putting it on.* The products we purchase, for the most part, are ones we've been conditioned to want, as we believe these will bring us a feeling of approval and admiration. And often they do, as well as making us feel happy and pleased with ourselves.

What about the people who seem to resist the conditioning: those who declare themselves against popular advertising, or the people who oppose cultural trends and claim to be a part of a counter-cultural group? Are they not conditioned to resist or oppose the conditioning? It is interesting to see many of the folks representing the counter-culture later rejoin the mainstream culture and actually promote it. For example, John McEnroe was the delinquent tennis champion who joined the establishment by becoming a tennis commentator and coach of the Davis Cup Team.

Conditioning is in everything we do and in everything we think about. The architecture of our homes is conditioned. We see in television programs the shift from the ranch style home of the 70s to the vaulted ceilings and spacious rooms of the 90s, and lately there appears to be a trend toward taking older homes with more character and renovating them to include exotic and expensive kitchens and bathrooms. Recently, I gave my niece a gift of a beautiful candle. As she commented over and over throughout the day on how much she appreciated it, I was surprised and pleased at how welcomed my gift was. Later, she confided in me that she had seen the candle in a television program that she watches and considered it very cool. Conditioning.

In each community you will find a chic hair salon at which is usually impossible to get an appointment. Is it possible that there exists in every community only one hairdresser who is the very best on earth? Or, is it simply that those hairdressers operate to satisfy the conditioned need of customers to be perceived as having the newest and most chic hairstyle? If you spend three times more than average to buy a baby's stroller with a name that has become the rage among young mothers, is that stroller three times as well built as all the others—or is it simply that the brand name denotes a certain superiority which the mothers want for their children?

We may judge these people, and pride ourselves in not being sucked into the materialistic, superficial world. Guess what? They are conditioned, just as we are conditioned. Of course, some conditioning is harmless, and other conditioning can cause real problems in our lives. While the power of suggestion to buy Pantene shampoo might not make a big difference in your life, it's important to recognize when conditioning is causing negativity in your life.

A client—I'll call her Lucy—came to see me when she began having problems with her ten-year-old son. She shared with me the atmosphere in the family and within her relationship with her husband. Lucy claimed her husband was psychologically abusive to her. She said he demeaned her and questioned everything she did, yet in his defense, she declared what a great father he was to their children, and praised him for not arguing in front of the children and being responsive to their needs. But she was miserable. She came to me to learn how to deal with the demeaning and insulting behavior she was now receiving from her son. Lucy claimed to be in the dark about how this problem originated. She was totally unaware that even though she and her husband were not arguing in front of their son, their son was being conditioned by his father's disparaging attitude toward his mother, and potentially toward all women. Before she could work on her relationship with her son, she needed to recognize that he was being conditioned by his father to act negatively toward her.

For those of you who are parents, you'll need to remember that you condition your children overtly, through direct communication and modeling, but you also condition your children covertly, through silent behaviors, non-verbal communications, and modeling. The conditioning occurs without the conscious intentions of the conditioners. For example, when a child begins to engage in problematic behaviors—such as dishonesty or disregard for others—that are also within the parent's character, the parent will often be mystified as to the origin of these behaviors, because he has yet to bring these behaviors to his own conscious awareness. Aspects of the conditioning—gestures, facial expressions, actions, reactions and remarks—are imparted without the parent's intention, or even awareness.

Before any of us can work through our conditioning or see how we condition other people, we need to recognize our problem areas. A problem is a blessing in that it clues us into an area of our lives that needs our attention.

WORKING WITH OUR CONDITIONING TO CHANGE OUR NEGATIVE REACTIONS

We are conditioned by our families, our social groups, our culture, and ourselves to spend a great deal of energy and time concerned with the way we look, and relatively little energy and time responding to how we feel physically. In many cases, we have been conditioned in such a way that we would rather look good than feel good. I hear people say, "If we would take care of our bodies half as well as we take care of our cars we would experience fewer health problems." I know for myself that it has taken a conscious commitment to address the conditioning within my life in order to stop reacting with unhealthy eating and exercising behaviors. I now practice how to listen to my body and respond to its needs rather than to make my body perform in order to fulfill my perceived, conditioned needs.

We are conditioned to compare ourselves to others, and even in our childhood stories we are taught to ask, "Mirror, mirror on the wall..." We want to conform to society's view of the ideal body type, and will do almost anything—including taking unhealthy and even dangerous measures—to lose inches around our waist or increase our biceps. We are conditioned to desire a certain body type and seek out liposuction, laser treatments, and all forms of cosmetic surgery in our attempts to have the body we have been conditioned to want. Amid heavy social conditioning, we go on diet regimens that haven't been fully proven. We exercise to the extent that we become injured, enlarge our heart, or become obsessed; all because we are conditioned to believe, "no pain, no gain."

A lot of people I encounter say, "Oh, you're so lucky to have a good metabolism," or, "You're lucky to be skinny. I bet you could eat anything." I was not lean as an adolescent. I began to think about my body when my brothers would bring their thin, beautiful girlfriends home when they were in high school. I really responded to the conditioning to be thin when my oldest brother told me on the way to the beach one day, "Adrianne, you should lose about ten pounds."

I responded so thoroughly to this conditioning that that was the last time he ever had to tell me to lose weight. I became an avid runner. From that point on I conditioned, and reinforced the conditioning, with regard to the shape of my body. I consciously conditioned myself into becoming a runner, even though I would dread the moment of running. Different parts of my body would become injured and I would push through the injury and continue running, learning to use ice and compression to allow me to continue conditioning my body. I would not listen to my body. I was so conditioned to want a thin, lean runner's body that I was willing to deny any communication from my body that it was becoming overly stressed.

I continued with my rigorous body conditioning, substituting other forms of exercise that I thought would be gentler on my body, like yoga and walking, still with the intention of maintaining the lean body that I achieved through running. I was still over-exercising. It wasn't until I injured myself in yoga that I could no longer deny that the manner in which I was conditioning my body was harming it. I could no longer avoid listening to my body. When I drank a lot of water, limited my sugar intake, lessened the amount of carbohydrates, and began eating more fruits and vegetables, my body responded better. Facing my conditioning on a deeper level also meant responding to the needs of my body with regard to exercise. My conditioned desire for a lean body lead me to Pilates, and what I discovered was that it required me to acknowledge the way I have been conditioning my body in order to begin the process of re-conditioning in a new, and more attentive manner: listening to my body. I could no longer push my body, and in fact pushing would not allow me to achieve the benefits I desired. Activities like long hikes and light yoga allowed me to stay in shape without overburdening my body.

The point I want to share is that even though I have begun to recondition myself to have an awareness of my body in a healthier and more respectful way, I still, on occasion, experience the suggestions of my youth to check myself out in a mirror or to push myself beyond my comfort zone. The old conditioning can still provoke a repetitive impulse. When the impulse arises to push myself unhealthily, I have to work through that experience—decondition the reaction—just as I have my clients do.

I will be sharing an exercise with you that I've done on corporate retreats to help workers to manage the stress and overwhelmed feelings they experience at work. You can use this exercise to deal with the stress of working against your negative conditioning, or any other stress that arises within you, causing feelings of being overwhelmed. Just as I turned to excessive exercise to avoid the feelings of shame about my body that I was conditioned to feel if I didn't look a certain way, many people turn to food to avoid their anxiety. Many comments are made at my retreats, but I will always remember when one of my workshop attendees once said, "You really helped me. I was not aware that my impulsive eating is a reaction to my inner feelings of anxiety that are being produced by my feeling of being overwhelmed as a result of my heavy workload. My conditioning is to eat whenever I experience difficult feelings such as anxiety, and you have taught me that by acknowledging the anxiety and working with it, I no longer have to react by eating." So many of us struggle with our eating habits without realizing we are eating to resolve emotional stress. As soon as this person did the breathing awareness exercise *Releasing Overwhelmed Feelings* she was able to see her conditioning clearly, and this acknowledgement gave her a sense of being able to change her reaction to the stress and eat more healthfully.

SNAP OUT OF IT NOW! MOMENT

Releasing Overwhelmed Feelings Using the Power of Breath Awareness

1. Settle into a comfortable and quiet space where you won't be disturbed.

2. Think of a time recently when you have experienced a sense of being overwhelmed.

3. Take a few minutes and try to bring that image to your mind.

4. Now, close your eyes and imagine yourself right back in that situation. Before we can shift a negative feeling sensation, we have to acknowledge and experience it within our body.

5. Still keeping your eyes closed, stay with this image. Describe how your body is feeling.

6. Where in your body do you feel the discomfort?

    • In your chest?

    • Your head?

    • Maybe your neck?

    • Perhaps your stomach?

7. Stay with this feeling sensation in your body.

8. If it's difficult to stay with this feeling, don't try to change it. Just acknowledge the challenge.

9. Shift your awareness to your breath. As you breathe, feel your breath moving in and out through your nose or mouth.

10. Feel, sense, your breath moving with your attention through your entire body.

11. Direct your breath to the area of your body that is uncomfortable.

12. Breathe to this area.

13. Imagine that as you inhale and exhale, your breath is going to this location.

14. Acknowledge the feeling sensation. The tightness in your chest. The racing feeling in your head. The pain in your neck. Whatever and wherever the sensation is for you.

15. As you breathe to the area of your body where the sensation is, experience the feeling for the first time.

16. What is your personal awareness of this feeling? If this is uncomfortable or difficult, don't try to change it, just acknowledge the discomfort or difficulty.

17. As you breathe to the feeling in your body, your breath will release the discomfort as you exhale. The feeling will dissipate.

18. As the disharmony within dissipates, notice how your body is feeling now. The body's natural rhythm is one of harmony.

19. When you are ready, gently open your eyes.

With this breathing awareness practice you can shift a pattern of disharmony—stress, anxiety, anger, overwhelmed feelings—within your body to one of balance and harmony. Allow yourself to use your inner balance to consciously choose your next action, rather than being controlled by your automatic reaction.

The body is where the feeling starts. The body is asking the mind for help with this feeling. An emotional reaction of fear is experienced in the mind, followed by attempts to calm the body. If rationalizations and denial don't work, then an overwhelmed feeling occurs.

With this exercise, you are learning to acknowledge and experience the feelings within your body. You are connecting with yourself, and are putting yourself in control of how you act and react. With practice, you will no longer be doomed to react with unhealthy, conditioned behaviors that are getting in your way of being the person you were meant to be.

FOUR STEPS TO ACCEPTING CONDITIONING

1. Recognition: Conditioning is a state of mind—a belief system—that is unconscious.

2. Acknowledgment: The way you think and interact is determined by your conditioning.

3. Awareness: Your conditioning is holding you back from fully experiencing the joy within yourself and the beauty in the world around you.

4. Freedom: With awareness of your conditioning, you begin to see that you can choose to Snap Out of It—your conditioned state of mind—Now! and begin living and breathing with awareness. You are free to become your own conditioner!

SNAP OUT OF IT NOW! MOMENT

Self-Observation

Take a few moments today and observe your interaction with two or three other people—your coworkers, boss, friends, the mailperson, grocery clerk, spouse, child, or whoever you may run into. As you observe, ask yourself the following questions:

1. Do I notice a change in the way I speak; the words I use or the tone in which I use them?

2. Do I make critical judgments of the person I'm talking with?

3. Do I have a change of attitude or behavior depending on the person I am with?

4. How authentic do I feel in each of these circumstances?

5. Am I playing a role?

Just notice how you interact with others. Later, when you are able take out your journal, go ahead and answer these questions. Feel free to spend some time journaling, as this is a great way to open up your awareness of yourself.

CHAPTER FIVE

Conditioned Identifications— The Emerging Uniqueness within the Conditioning

We identify with parts of all the conditioning present within our environment—thoughts, judgments, beliefs, expectations, and ways of behaving. These are *conditioned identifications*. To experience life fully and with inner joy we will bring these C-Is to awareness.

We humans are extraordinary, emotional animals. Like other animals, humans are conditioned to act in a certain way. But unlike other animals, we have the capacity to become conscious of ourselves, our thinking and our interactions. With conscious awareness, we can awaken to our conditioned state of mind, and begin making choices for ourselves that are congruent with our deeper, intuitive nature.

As discussed in the last chapter, our environment causes the formation of conditioned identifications in our minds throughout our lives. This process takes place without our conscious awareness or active participation. Our emotional reactions, which are internally linked with our survival instinct, send neurological messages to us, causing discomfort or incongruity when our conditioning turns negative or conflicts with our desires. Our unconscious minds often attempt to resolve internal stress or contradiction by using the network of rules, beliefs, and truths whereby we function in everyday life—our conditioning. However, this blocks the flow of our emotions. Since the body and our thoughts and emotions are all linked, unresolved blockage causes everything from physical to emotional to neurological damage. We are not aware of the enormous impact that our conditioning has upon our lives, from the people we associate with to the state of our health. Such is the power of our mind and its conditioning that we have the power to make ourselves sick or make ourselves well.

My method is about helping you break free from your negative conditioned identifications so that you can experience physical well-being and inner joy. You're reading this book because you want to make better choices for yourself, and you need help. One stumbling block is that most of us believe that we are capable of making choices that are not influenced by our conditioning. The reality is that the neurological pathways that construct our system of internal rules and regulations—our conditioning—are the solid roads on which our choices are made. From birth, our conditioners program us. The beliefs and models of behaviors from our parents, friends, schools, churches, societies and cultures are subconsciously instilled in us. Our tacit acceptance of the world we live in makes us the unwitting reinforcers of our own programming. Each time we engage our conditioned thoughts, perceptions, and judgments, our conditioned identifications, we are actively and unconsciously re-conditioning our programming. And yet, we are continually frustrated when we are unable to change. This frustration stems from the fact that we react without conscious awareness. We don't know that we are trapped within our conditioning, and we find ourselves yelling at our spouse, or predicting and manifesting a negative outcome for ourselves. Over and over, we find ourselves proclaiming, "There I go again," or "I can't believe this happens to me all the time," or we may deny our reaction altogether. We are driving on autopilot, and it's time to Snap Out of It Now!

This chapter is about recognizing the conditioning agents that are creating the mental paths we don't want to follow, so that we can take charge at the wheel and navigate our own pathway to success! On that note, I'm going to start you off with a self-affirmation exercise to prime the pump. *Stop, look,* and *listen* to yourself and your environment. Now, say these self-affirmations aloud five times each before moving forward with this chapter.

SNAP OUT OF IT NOW! MOMENT

Accept Yourself and Activate Your Positive Thinking!

1. I acknowledge that I am conditioned.

2. I accept myself as who I am.

3. I am confident and self-assured.

4. I am capable.

5. I am breaking free from the limitations of my conditioning.

6. I have the power to make good choices for myself.

7. I am as important as anyone else, and my needs are just as important as those of other people.

8. I can decide what's best for me.

9. I can do it—anything that I can imagine for myself I can make a reality.

LET'S WAKE UP!

You have the ability to be aware of your conditioned self. With that awareness, you will be capable of truly creating the life that is right for you. To do so, I am going to provide you with the tools you need to consciously choose how you react to circumstances, people, and events in your life.

To start with, let's take a look at ourselves—our conditioned identifications—and awaken to the conditioned nature of our lives. Life is a journey and on this journey there are plenty of twists and turns and pitfalls. Don't be held back by limiting beliefs instilled in you by others. Smooth out your ride by taking the reins and confronting your conditioned belief system. Then, you can focus on the conditioning that is destructive and inhibits your ability to create the life you want.

Chapter 9, "Acknowledgment and Acceptance of Our Conditioning," is specifically designed to guide you through your confrontation with your conditioned identifications. For now, let's continue with the process of self-awareness. I do not believe there to be any external power—negative forces in the Universe or an unforgiving God—that compels us to continue doing things that are self-destructive or self-denying. Our task as human beings is to come to greater self-awareness and discover for ourselves the path to inner joy—the birthright of all human beings. I have used the term sleepwalking to help you understand that within the conditioning we are limited with regard to our choice of actions. In order to be free to make conscious choices for ourselves, we need to wake up! It is this process of waking up that I have written about here, and waking up from the conditioning is the essence of the Snap Out of It Now! method.

It is amazing how unawake we are! Aren't you still making choices that you really don't want to make, and don't you continue to find yourself in circumstances and situations in life in which you really don't want to be? Well, keep reading—I am going to show you how to break these unwanted cycles.

You may or may not be aware of a specific conditioned pattern instilled in you. Most of us are unaware that we cannot change a conditioned behavior—blaming, eating, drinking, procrastinating, or self-criticizing—simply by deciding to change it. The only method of breaking free from our negative conditioned patterns of thinking and reacting is by first observing and experiencing these negative patterns. Conditioned behavior is linked to emotions within the body, and until we add to our awareness, the conscious acknowledgment and experience of the underlying emotions, we will continue thinking and reacting according to our program. No change will be experienced.

You have to know what you want to change before you can change it!

With a little effort, we can understand where our thinking stems from and we can figure out why we react the way we do, but we still come back to the fact that we continue to act and react in the same problematic, self-destructive, and dispassionate ways. We don't know how to pause or stop the cycle of reactions.

One client, Mark, wanted to change the way he reacted toward his wife. He knew that his aggressive and insulting behavior was destructive to their relationship, as well as being a negative influence on his daughter. I helped Mark understand that his offensive behavior was an automatic reaction stemming from his own conditioned identification with inadequacy, accompanied by a fear of falling short at work and in life. Mark had left a high-level position with a successful company to open his own business, and he was absolutely terrified of failure. The first thing we worked on was his relationship, because without his wife and family he felt the success of his business would be irrelevant.

I guided him in becoming aware of emotions, and then specifically aware of when feelings of fear would arise in his body. Mark began to recognize this feeling of fear as the feeling that he had just before starting an argument with his wife. When he engaged the angry reaction, he felt an emotional release and therefore no longer felt the uncomfortable sensation of fear, but his cathartic outbursts were ruining his personal relationships. I helped him understand that the reaction of anger had become a conditioned reaction to the inner emotion of fear. The reaction was engaged in order to protect and distance Mark from his fear. In this conditioned process, his attention shifted outside himself and away from the inner fear where his conditioning told him that he could resolve the emotion. Mark had never acknowledged or experienced the feeling of fear, and therefore it unconsciously continued to feed his cycle of anger and aggressiveness. As Mark began to accept that his thoughts of inadequacy were conditioned beliefs that were provoking deep-seated feelings of fear, he was able to de-condition the reaction.

Don't forget, it's just as important to acknowledge the positive conditioning that works for you. Just as negative thoughts can impact and interfere with your ability to excel in areas of your life, actively engaging positive thinking can allow you to bring possibilities that previously might have been beyond imagination into your experience and your life. The trouble is, we get so stuck in what we perceive as our lives that we can't find any way out! We allow the negative thinking—a conditioned pattern in the majority of human beings—to dominate our experience. Wake up! Realize that you can break out of the negativity and focus on what is positive within you! The ability to self-motivate is a learned behavior that requires practice, and then more practice. Positive reinforcement, self-praise, and self-encouragement will help you to move forward with your journey in a confident, meaningful way.

SNAP OUT OF IT NOW! MOMENT

Positive Thinking

1. Stop manifesting, through your negative thinking, what you do not want for yourself!

2. Start creating, through positive and self-expansive assertions, the life of your dreams.

Remember the focused intention I asked you to create for yourself in chapter 3? Well, now I ask that you create five positive and self-expansive assertions that are congruent with your focused intention. As you write down your assertions, make sure to write them in the present tense. It is important that when you read them out loud that it is clear to you that you are in the process of actualizing them, not hoping or wanting them to come true. And, don't be afraid to be boastful. This is your life, and only you can fill it with excellence and joy!

As an example, a client of mine created an intention: to qualify for the PGA Tour. His positive assertions were the following:

1. I am an excellent golfer.

2. I have confidence in my swing.

3. I am fearless on the golf course.

4. I love my short game.

5. I feel exhilarated by the challenge of competition.

Okay, you've got the idea. NOW—it's your turn!

My Self-Expansive Assertions

1. _____

2. _____

3. _____

4. _____

5. _____

Say each statement out loud to yourself five times! Make the act of speaking these assertions aloud a part of your daily routine. You are what you think about, so start conditioning yourself with positive and expansive thinking!

HOW DO CONDITIONED IDENTIFICATIONS WORK?

As young children we are conditioned to want to meet the needs of those whom we love—our core conditioners, usually our parents. We strive to meet the expectations we perceive, and as we grow older our core conditioners' expectations become our own. Now, you probably can't change the fact that you have grown to love chocolate mint ice cream, or prefer watching ice skating to bob-sledding during the Winter Olympics, but you can change your path in life.

Think about how you interact with your environment, with people, with your job, and with yourself. Don't try to create a scenario of your perfect dream self. For example, let's say Betty goes on a hike and finds herself consumed by thoughts in her head. She seeks to change her behavior by joining the Sierra Club with the hope that she will become a more attentive hiker and learn from fellow hikers how to appreciate nature more fully. When she completes a hike with her new group, Betty complains that the folks in the club are boring. They take too long to discuss one shrub, or are just not her kind of people. The hikes take too long, and she doesn't feel that she's getting enough targeted exercise.

My point is, you can try to change your life and change how you experience your life, but trying to be different from who you are will not override your conditioned identifications. You can't just decide that you will begin to enjoy nature walks and listen to discussions of a rare bush when you get pleasure from going to the local gym for aerobics and are conditioned to exercise as a means to an end. Work with what you've got: work with your conditioned identifications to make your life better for you. Don't try to change yourself into someone you're not—it will never work!

For example, when Bess was in elementary school, her mother was always available to help her with her homework. Her temperament reflected characteristics of diligence and conscientiousness, and therefore she had a strong desire to complete the homework and to complete it to the best of her ability. Bess's mother, in her efforts to help, would talk with her about what she was going to write. The trouble was that Bess thought what her mother was saying was so good that afterwards she would write out what her mom had said, rather than using her own words. The exchange with her mother was so stimulating and exciting that both enjoyed this experience, with the result that Bess would arrive back from school with an A paper. Unfortunately, instead of trying to develop her own voice, Bess was just imitating her mother and trying to be someone she wasn't.

It never worked. Once her mother wasn't there for her to copy-cat, Bess still wrote successfully, but she had developed the complexes—misleading conditioned beliefs—that her own writing didn't have value, that she was incapable of articulating herself, and that her ideas didn't have value. In Bess's mind, to be a good writer she had to be her mother, and write what her mother would write. Despite strong grades, Bess felt she needed help from others to accomplish self-expressive tasks. Bess felt embarrassed at the thought of anyone reading her work. Using the Snap Out of It Now! method to acknowledge and experience her inner fear, Bess was able to break free from the trappings of those conditioned identifications and validate her own voice.

Look around yourself and you will see that people react differently to the same situation. Why is it that one person might react with distaste at the idea of dating an older or younger person, while someone else does not look at age as even a consideration for going out with someone? We could ask ourselves, *How did I form this conditioned identification that older, or younger, men/women are not desirable as dating partners, and why did I form it?* We could spend all day long figuring this out—and probably everything we come up with will be correct—but we will continue with the nagging thought that there is still something more. The reason for this nagging thought is plain and simple: we are conditioned. You may have identified with conditioning to dating people of your own age, and whenever you think of dating a younger or older person you will have a visceral, conditioned response. You might go on a date with a gorgeous person ten years younger, or meet an amazing older person whom you really like, and tell yourself that this conditioned identification is really not that significant, only to realize that these thoughts and reactions have become a part of who you are and what you want. You will still struggle with your core conditioned identifications, but with awareness you can make choices that will be more congruent with your chosen path in life.

We often limit ourselves and close ourselves off to the possibilities that lie beyond our conditioned identifications by boxing ourselves into certain modes of thinking and reacting. A client of mine who is gay would describe situations that would seem unbearable for any heterosexual person. He openly shared with me that when he goes into certain restaurants with his partner, they are treated not only with distaste, but are often ignored and have to leave without being served. This may seem an extreme example of a negative identification where the employees of the restaurant are boxed into their negative thinking, but don't fool yourself—it happens all the time! We might identify with the religious conditioning to which we've been exposed, so that these conditioned identifications close us off from listening to the views of other religions. We might identify with the conditioned perceptions of our family and friends toward other people and ways of living, and as a result of these conditioned identifications we limit ourselves from opportunities to join in relationship with someone who does not fit within our familiar and comfortable conditioned perceptions.

What about the positive labels we give ourselves—those conditioned identifications that are responsible for creating and reinforcing our positive self-image? We can each identify beliefs we have about ourselves, and labels that we have given ourselves, and recognize the feeling of pride that emerges following engagement with these conditioned identifications. Maybe you're a good athlete, and the label of good athlete allows you to feel good about yourself. Maybe you're the smart child, or the artistic type. A positive conditioned identification for me is, *I am a good skier.* I learned when I was young, and then became really good during my graduate work. Skiing provided a wonderful opportunity to get away from my studies and take a break from my academic concerns. It also allowed me to return to my work refreshed and energized. I still identify myself as a good skier and get a lot of satisfaction and joy from this identification—it works for me! Each of us has some conditioned identifications that serve us well and seem to guide us positively toward experiences of success or pride. If it works well for you, then the conditioned identification is positive. Just as we can use the power of our breath to de-condition a negative reaction, we can use the breath to reinforce positive experiences.

Problems arise when you do something you've been conditioned to do that is destructive to you. You might say to yourself, *Why do I keep getting myself into that situation?* You repeat these destructive behaviors because your conditioned identification tells you that your needs will be met, even if they aren't. The power of the conditioning overshadows your repressed cognizance of what the unfortunate consequences of your behavior might be. Here are some examples:

- The heavy drinker finds some satisfaction in altered self-awareness as the drink affects the mind, and does not consider the terrible effects on his family when he becomes abusive as a result of his drinking.

- The people who have habitual difficulty paying the mortgage each month continue to go on spending sprees because their conditioning tells them that they will experience euphoria through the process of spending money.

- The serial adulterer may love and need her spouse but be incapable of resisting the allure of the temporary excitement of shared desire.

All of these people may only come out of their destructive patterns when they recognize them for what they are—conditioned identifications and conditioned reactions. The negative effect on their lives alone does not enable recognition. Rather, awareness of the conditioned identifications that cause the reaction enables recognition of the cycle and enables them to stop engaging the cycle.

FINDING YOUR VOICE WITHIN THE CONDITIONED IDENTIFICATIONS

All of us want to feel safe, happy, and satisfied with life, and we habitually follow patterns set by our conditioning in order to achieve this satisfaction. When we do something that we've been conditioned to do and do it well, we feel good about ourselves. Our contentment is contingent upon where we've set our expectations. As we meet the needs of a conditioned identification that is congruent with our deeper nature, we feel soothed, comfortable with the road we are traveling, and we feel that we know where we are headed. We can be more relaxed and less irritable in our social and professional interactions. Feeling safe and congruent within our conditioning, we are more patient with ourselves and listen more easily to others, because our internal criteria for safety are met.

Conversely, when our conditioned needs are not met, we can become distracted and disconnected from ourselves. Fearful of wrongdoing, we find ourselves absorbed in self-critical thoughts and rationalizations. We continue playing our society's reindeer games. We feel good about being a part of something greater than ourselves, something we share with others.

When the initial feelings of incongruity are experienced, it is not uncommon for us to feel that we must conform whether it feels right or not. Going against a core conditioned identification for the first time is not easy and may be frightening, so we may react according to a conditioned identification. When we decide to step outside of the conditioning, or to play according to the program no longer, we are breaking the mold that all of those we love are continuing to live by. The belief that we are now on our own, without the love and support of our conditioners, will lead to sensations that we are shrinking and our world is becoming smaller and smaller. The irony here is that our world is on the verge of expanding beyond our dreams. These sensations of fear often provoke what I call the rubber band effect—feelings of incongruity with the conditioning provoke a desire to step away, and then our conditioned reactions stemming from inner fear of being alone yank us right back into the box of our conditioning.

For Freida, this sensation was initially experienced when she began to say no to expectations from her significant others—even when her no was accepted comfortably. Her perception of her conditioning was such that she should always say yes. The power our conditioned identifications have over us is so strong that when we do not immediately conform to them, we experience feelings of abandonment and fear that the love we receive from others will be taken from us. These lead us back into our negative conditioning so that we can feel safe again.

While living within the box of your conditioning, you will probably feel that this is the only reality possible for you, and that there is no alternative reality. If you accept that change is possible, you might feel consumed by feelings of failure when you rebel against the conditioned identifications that are problematic. We are so set in our ways,—our conditioned identifications—that if we change anything in our lives, it's easy to feel we have failed or that we will be rejected. Here is an exercise to help you when you have broken down a wall of a conditioned identification and seen beyond it. There will be tough times when you feel unsure and you consider going back to your old ways, even though they've hurt you before. You may suddenly feel frightened of standing on your own.

SNAP OUT OF IT NOW! MOMENT

Staying Strong—Staying Connected

All of us need to maintain a strong connection with our intention and our dream for life. If we don't have a clear picture of how we want to live and with whom, where we want to live, and what we intend to achieve, then we will never live it.

1. Ask yourself these questions:

2. What do you see as your unique gift?

3. How do you use your creativity, talent, and gift?

4. Do you feel content with who you are?

5. How satisfied are you with yourself:

   - Physically?

   - Intellectually?

   - Emotionally?

   - Sexually?

   - Spiritually?

   - Socially?

   - Professionally?

6. What is most important to you in life?

7. Are you living the life you want to live?

8. What is missing in your life?

9. What are you doing when you feel the most inner joy?

> Now, spend some time with your journal. Write out your answers to these questions, and then allow yourself to continue writing within your stream of consciousness. This exercise will help you clarify what you want and guide you in making a choice—to stand true to yourself and continue on the path to becoming your own conditioner, or to step back into the comfort and security of your conditioning, whether it serves the greater part of you or not.

DON'T LET YOUR CONDITIONED IDENTIFICATIONS HOLD YOU BACK!

Conditioned identifications are the labels we give ourselves. David's parents conditioned him to believe that he would achieve great things in life. Together with his conditioned identification with greatness came other labels like lazy and unmotivated, the things he would call himself whenever he couldn't meet what he perceived as his parents' expectations of him. His reaction? He conditioned himself to make excuses for why his greatness wasn't evident, such as *I'm lazy and therefore my greatness does not blossom; I'm unmotivated and therefore I sit around waiting for the greatness to emerge.* David felt intimidated by the challenge of trying to become what he believed his parents would deem great.

Many children are told they are special and great, and we are all special and unique—but owning our true gift may be difficult within our perceived expectations of others. Getting caught up in trying to meet lofty expectations of our parents often leaves us feeling imprisoned in the life design we have created as a result of our conditioning, and overly frustrated with our failures. When something goes wrong, we know it's wrong to blame someone else, and yet we're all too ready to blame ourselves. Don't play the blame game at all! We all make mistakes. Begin to learn from the mistakes you make while following your own intuitive design for life!

As David confronted his conditioning, he realized that lazy and unmotivated were the labels he was giving himself whenever he was not actualizing what he perceived as greatness. When he looked further within himself, he was able to identify deep feelings of fear within his body that provoked the need to blame himself for not living up to his perception of greatness. From here David enabled himself to connect with the feelings of fear using the power of the breath. I coached David to stay with the sensations of fear, without engaging the stories in his head associated with the fear. I had him focus his breathing on this area of the body. When David learned to breathe away the sensations of fear, then he began to hear and understand what he needed for himself to truly experience greatness within, breaking through the wall of his conditioning and finding his true voice. In moving on to actualize the life he wanted for himself, he began to create his own definitions of greatness.

SELF-PERCEPTION VS. SELF-ACTUALIZATION

I had another client, Maureen, who described herself as a woman who was "not easily liked by others." She perceived that when she engaged another person socially and felt a connection, afterwards, that person would not like her or want to see her again. As a child, Maureen felt lost in the mix of gregarious and rather aggressive siblings, and always felt that she had to fight for attention and acknowledgment. It doesn't take a genius to see how she developed the conditioned identifications that she was uninteresting, boring, inconsequential, and unmemorable.

In stark contrast, Maureen perceived herself at work as having the respect and admiration of the people with whom she worked. She felt capable of establishing good working relationships with colleagues, and perceived them to enjoy her company. Professionally, Maureen perceived that others viewed her as intelligent, conscientious, and enthusiastic, and more than a few times, she shared, she had been told that she was perceived as a powerful woman. Socially, she perceived that others viewed her as too serious, and not friendly enough, boring, and unmemorable.

Why, she wondered, was the perception she had of herself in one arena different from the perception she had of herself in another arena? Why, when she felt competent in one moment, would the feeling totally dissipate and morph into a feeling of being inconsequential?

My client's identity as a professional businesswoman allowed her to feel self-confident at work. She was conditioned by her professional education and training to be competent as a businesswoman, and she reacted to this conditioning with feelings of self-worth. When she changed environments, her other self-identification as uninteresting would trigger internal feelings of worthlessness. As a result, she would distance herself from others socially, declining social offers from coworkers and staying home on the weekends. This led to feelings of loneliness, which only fed her sense of unworthiness. Maureen learned to de-condition her negative social reactions and began to condition herself to join others socially and to feel more at ease with them.

Today, Maureen is conscious that she must keep these underlying feelings of unworthiness in check so that she can maintain a connection with her own self-worth and feel the freedom not to engage her conditioned reaction.

My client is not alone with regard to her intra-psychic pattern of disapproval and disappointment. Many actors cannot read reviews and critiques of their work or watch videos of themselves. There are writers who write with a bag over their head. Some beautiful women are unable to accept a compliment. There are corporate executives who are never satisfied with their achievements and continue seeking more and more power. From our earliest experiences we, as human beings, have been conditioned to feel dissatisfied with ourselves. Much of this dissatisfaction has its roots in our early childhood interpretations of the messages of our conditioning. The understanding that many of the problems we face in life stem from conflicts within the conditioning—our own and that of others—and the acceptance and confrontation with our conditioned identifications, will lead us to greater self-awareness and self-love.

In the next chapter, we will discuss how to forge your own path in life despite your conditioning. In the meantime, let's focus on the self-acceptance within a particular conditioned identification. When I first began to wake up to my conditioning, I choose a lightweight conditioned identification to become familiar with: I believed I was intellectually inferior to my older brother and I reacted to this belief by clamming up when he asked me a serious question. I came to recognize and accept that my negative reaction to my brother caused my subsequent feelings of self-doubt and embarrassment, my need to make a joke out of my incompetence, and eventually, my self-degradation. Once I was aware of this cycle of reactions, and was able to accept it rather then deny it out of humiliation, I was capable of working with it and eventually de-conditioning my reaction. Today, rather than clamming up, I am more likely to challenge my brother on his opinion! In a later chapter you will learn to de-condition the reaction, but for now I'd like you to simply experience and become familiar with the conditioning—your ways thinking and reacting.

SNAP OUT OF IT NOW! MOMENT

Accepting a Conditioned Identification

1. Recognize a conditioned identification—belief, expectation, or self-judgment—that is getting you down.

   My conditioned identification: _____

   _____

2. How do you feel when you speak this conditioned identification out loud?

   _____

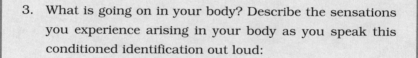

3. What is going on in your body? Describe the sensations you experience arising in your body as you speak this conditioned identification out loud:

    _____

    _____

    Now, take a moment to take care of yourself. Become aware of your breathing. Breathe to the sensation within your body, wherever it may be. Feel your breath connecting with the sensation as you inhale, and then feel the sensation dissipate as you exhale.

4. If you feel ready (if not, you can come back to this later), describe here or in your journal how you typically react when this conditioned identification is activated in your life experience. Allow yourself to bring this conditioned identification back to your awareness and visualize how you react in your thinking, feeling, and doing.

    _____

    _____

5. Now, congratulate yourself! You are waking up to your conditioning, turning off the cruise control, and becoming your own conditioner. You are courageous, honest, and on your way to experiencing inner joy!

In this process, as well as all the other exercises I offer in this book, feel free to turn to your friends for support. There's nothing like your best friend, mother, father, boyfriend, girlfriend, or confidante to help you stay on track. And if none of them feels right to you, there is no shame in going to a counselor or therapist for help. If you need additional support and unbiased opinions, using the resources available to you is the strong thing to do.

CHAPTER SIX

Working with Your Conditioned Identifications to Forge Your Own Life Path

W e cannot define the *mystery*—infinity, the exquisite order of the universe, and the meaning of life—we *can* identify negative conditioned identifications that stop us from seeing the beauty within ourselves. In doing so, we open ourselves to the mystery of life!

CHOOSING A PATH IN LIFE

All those built-up expectations, social rules, and voices of your peers affect both who you are and what career path you choose. People become teachers, lawyers, salespeople, professional athletes, writers, nurses or doctors, or inherit the family business and when some of them come home at night they kick the damn dog! That's conditioning. Now maybe you don't beat on old Fido, but you might be angry without knowing what you're angry about. You might be dissatisfied at work because instead of choosing a career or life path, you feel you've fallen into one. Your career might even take on a life of its own and start to condition you to think and act differently. You may be satisfied in your work, and yet feel bullied by conditioned voices telling you that you should be further along and accomplishing more. Does this sound familiar?

You may remain as a teacher, lawyer, nurse, or salesperson until you retire, and then realize that you had no passion for—or may even have truly hated—whatever job you chose. During the years you worked at this job you thought of running away, changing your job, or just lying in bed and never going to work again. What we don't realize is that we become trapped within our conditioned identifications—we can't see any way out because all we see is the conditioning. Every day that you went to work, you reinforced this conditioned identification until it became second nature and immune to any questioning.

Some of you may be thinking, *I don't agree with this. I definitely feel that I have participated with my choice of career and I am aware of my choices.* If you feel content and pleased with your career choice, then the point I am making here may be moot. However, if you are not happy in your work and fantasize about doing something else, or about retirement, then this section will be relevant to you. I am not suggesting or wanting to imply that you change careers in order to become happy with life. I am suggesting and wanting to convey that when you become aware of your conditioned identifications and how they are impacting the way you engage your career, you are suddenly back in control of your life and how you experience it!

With awareness of your conditioned identifications, your true self, your deeper and intuitive nature, comes the opportunity to participate with your conditioning. Remember there are many conditioned identifications that are working for you. I do not want you to throw the baby out with the bath water. I do want you to learn how to participate and work with your conditioned identifications. This is what I mean by becoming your own conditioner: you become able to choose which conditioned truths work for you and are life enhancing, and which ones you need to break free from and re-condition. Let's start off with a journaling exercise.

Begin to confront your conditioned identifications that are influencing your work experience.

Your Path

Pull out your trusty journal and spend some time with these questions:

1. Do you feel that you were aware of choosing your career?

2. What choices did you consider?

3. Do you feel that the choice was yours, or was it influenced by others?

4. Do you presently feel pleased with your choice?

5. Can you recognize the conditioned identifications that are determining how you engage your career?

    • Are you consumed with vague feelings of doubt and angst?

    • Do you feel inspired and optimistic in your career?

    • Are you feeling trapped and without options?

    • Are you connected with your career and do you feel you are making a difference?

    • Do you believe that others are smarter and more capable than you?

See if you can spot other conditioned identifications that are associated with your work experience. For example, some common ones are: I have no choice; I'll never be happy in this job; I don't have the talent to be really successful; or, conversely, No one truly appreciates my talents; I am not being respected as I should be.

Some of you may feel lucky enough that your conditioning has led you into life situations that allow you to meet the needs of your conditioned identifications—to become a successful architect, dentist, plumber, or technician—and you may feel satisfied and content. When we live the program that has been set for us and we are acknowledged for our success, we feel good. We feel self-fulfilled, if even for just a moment. The irony may be that we are living the program successfully in our field, and yet feeling unfulfilled because our conditioning has confined us to the box of whatever field we have chosen. While traveling to India this year, I sat next to a very successful businessman. After our nap, we began to visit. I shared that I had just written a book, *Snap Out of It Now!*, and was in the process of shopping it to publishers. After giving him the 30-second pitch, he told me that he feels that he is living within a golden prison. He said his cell is certainly beautiful, the meals are great, and he even gets to spend time in lovely gardens—but a prison nevertheless. He described his life as being completely controlled by his schedule, which, he said, was not even arranged by him. His life is scheduled down to the minute, and is planned out for more than a year. Even though he loves his work, he said he has no freedom to decide, for example, to take the day off and spend it with his son. Before we arrived in India, he told me he would love to learn how to Snap Out of It Now! I told him I would send him a copy upon publication.

Do you feel like there are things you want to do in your life that are simply impossible? Maybe you love your work, like my flight companion, but feel you controlled by your schedule? Maybe you want to take an art class, but you've always been told you aren't artistic. Maybe you want to play a musical instrument, but your friends scoff at the thought of you in your Wall Street suit and a clarinet, taking fifteen-minute breaks from your 80-hour workweek to toot on the roof. Maybe you want to join a book group, but never allow yourself time away from your kids because the babysitter's too expensive and nobody else does things quite like you do. Or maybe you want to settle down and get married, but your single friends always expect you to have the flavor of the week on your arm. Give yourself a break. Your conditioning is not allowing you to integrate aspects of your true self such as interest in artistic design, music, literature, or a desire for deeply satisfying personal relationships. We cannot begin to participate actively in our choices until we become aware of our conditioned identifications that interfere with our ability to make conscious decisions.

SNAP OUT OF IT NOW! MOMENT

Listen to Your Heart

1. Take a moment for yourself. Put this book down. Sitting right where you are, find a comfortable position.

2. Become aware of your breathing.

3. Focus on your breathing until you find a comfortable and still space within your body.

4. If you feel sensations of discomfort, spend a few minutes focusing your breathing on the area of discomfort. As you exhale, breathe the discomfort away.

5. When you are feeling quiet and still, imagine that you are an actor with a script that you have taken on and have accepted. You play your role admirably.

---

6. After playing the role for some time, you start to realize there may be a better way to play the role.

   - What would it feel like to change some of the lines?

   - Are you afraid to alter the script?

   - What would happen if you did change the script?

   - Could you see yourself defying the traditional script put before you?

   - What would it feel like to start writing your own script?

7. You are the star of the show! You have the right to do what makes you happy. Sure you will feel fear—but fear is not the signal to stop. The experience of fear is usually the sign that we are close to something that is very important to us. *Stop*, *look*, and *listen* to the sensation of fear within your body. Now, *breathe* to the sensation and allow the fear to guide you.

Your world and your understanding of yourself have been conditioned, but you don't have to follow or conform to this conditioned reality. You can listen to your heart and make conscious decisions that are not directed by the script of your life written by somebody else. This exercise reminds me of a quote from Nietzsche, "The less men are fettered by tradition, the greater becomes the inward activity of their motives."

Here are several stories that illustrate how our conditioned identifications can hold us back.

I Enjoy My Work, but There Is Something Missing

A 58-year old man came to see me after being referred by his family practitioner. Henry, we'll call him, owned a plumbing contracting business. His reason for seeking help was that he had difficulty sleeping, had constant headaches, and his wife described him as "uncharacteristically irritable". His physician, taking into consideration his age, referred him to a neurologist to calm his fear of a brain tumor. He came to me with a clean bill of health. As we began talking, he shared his dream of having his son join him in the family plumbing business. He told me how he looked forward to having the sign over his business read *Father and Son Plumbing*. About a year and half ago his son asked to join him in the business, which naturally pleased Henry. Henry said that recently, his son had started to become angry when they were working together on a contract and had begun to force his opinion with regard to the contract even in the presence of the customers.

Henry was confused by his behavior and didn't know how to deal with him. He shared with me that his son was living with a lovely young woman and planning to get married. Henry and his wife were delighted. He talked about raising his son, and how much joy they had together when Henry brought him along on the job. His son would climb under the houses, and when with his friends, he would often pretend to be a plumber in their play. The anger from his son could not come as more of a surprise to Henry. In the past few months, his son had also begun coming to work late. He would leave early from time to time to meet his girlfriend, and take mental health days. Henry says that his son's quality of work, and the way he deals with other employees, is outstanding.

The history Henry gave me suggested that his son was experiencing a conflict within his conditioning. His son had no problems moving out of the home and finding a place of his own; he was in a relationship that was leading to marriage and a family; he was planning on purchasing a home; and his work was of excellent quality. The anger that Henry described, as well as the showing up late, leaving work early, and the mental health days all led me to suspect that there was something he was unable to express. Given the quality of life described in the other areas of his life, I suspected the issue related to his choice of career, which was conditioned. I told Henry that it would be important for me to see his son and asked him what he thought of this. He said that his son had told him that he would like to come and see me.

A meeting was set up for the son, Sam. He shared that he was not sure why he had so much anger when working with his father. He said he loved his father and respected him as a plumber. And yet, he said no matter how hard he tried, he continued to feel angry and to raise his voice when negotiating a contract alongside his father. I asked Sam to tell me what he thought was going on with himself. At first he claimed he had no idea. Then, he said he realized that even though he enjoyed the work of being a plumber and enjoyed being with his father and seeing how happy his father was to have him in the business, he felt there was something missing for him in his work. He said he had always wanted to do something more creative, something that would allow him to express himself. Then, he said to me, "This might sound crazy to you, but I have always wanted to be an actor. And the craziest thing of all is that I don't have a problem with being a plumber. I have felt like a plumber since I was a kid. I just don't seem to be able to shake the feeling of wanting to be an actor. I think about it all the time."

Here was my dilemma as a therapist. I realized that I had a responsibility to both father and son, as I knew that the relationship between the father and son was very important for Sam and will continue to be so for the rest of his life. I saw that the conditioning within this family was toward Sam becoming a plumber. His father was a plumber, and the family business was plumbing, Sam pretended to be plumber as a child, and Sam's relationship with his father began with their joy together as plumbers. I saw that Sam had identified with being a plumber. Sam did not feel forced by his father to come into the family business; he said that he chose to come into the business. What is clear is that Sam believed that as a result of his free will, he made the choice to go into business with his father and to become a plumber.

I said, "Sam, if you chose to go into the business, how come you haven't chosen to leave the business and become the actor you have always wanted to be?" He responded, "Every time I think about leaving the business I feel I would be disappointing my father. And then, I realize that my father has always told me he wants me to do what I want to do. I don't know why I can't leave and pursue acting."

Sam identified himself as a plumber, and without him being aware of it, his childhood conditioning influenced his choice to come into the family business. The conditioned identification that directed Sam into choosing the family business had multiple processes: thoughts, feelings, and sensations. Sam always admired his father. He felt secure with income from plumbing. He felt confident and competent with plumbing work. Sam followed the path that he began as a young child, and felt a real self-worth and a sense of mastery from following this path.

The anger Sam displayed by showing up late, leaving early, and taking mental health days were all reactions to his confusion as to why he chose to be a plumber, and yet still felt that something was missing. He believed that he was free to choose his path, but his conditioned identifications determined his choice.

This is what we don't realize. We identify with our conditioning, and each choice we make is made within the conditioned identification. I realize how difficult it might be for you to not know what happened with Sam, so I'll share the conclusion here. Sam came to accept that his conditioning was to become a plumber and work with his father. He discovered that he didn't want to change these conditioned identifications; to a great extent they were working for him. He did decide to pursue his idea of taking an acting class in the evenings. While Sam was reacting with anger and avoidance of work, he was totally unable to consider an option like this. When we confront our conditioned identifications, as Sam did, and we listen to our feelings and see what they are pointing us toward, we become aware of choices and opportunities to which we were previously blind. In Sam's case, the anger was alerting Sam to his denial of something important within himself. The truth is, life is simple—the conditioning attempts to make it complex. When the obvious is seen, we doubt it.

SNAP OUT OF IT NOW! MOMENT

Breathing Awareness Exercise: Awareness of Feelings

- Do you feel something is missing in your life?

- Do you feel discontent with a part of yourself or with the choices you've made?

- Do you find yourself angry and resentful, and don't know why?

- Do you feel frightened and at the same time ironically drawn toward taking some action in your career or with life in general?

In her book *The Way of Woman*, Helen Luke writes, "Each of us, as we journey through life, has the opportunity to find and to give his or her unique gift. Whether that gift is great or small in the eyes of the world does not matter at all—not at all; it is through the finding and the giving that we may come to know the joy that lies at the center of both the dark times and the light."

The conditioned voices in our heads will cloud and distort how we perceive our gift and our purpose in life. Life begins when we awaken to ourselves! When we begin to identify and experience our feelings and let our feelings show us our truth.

1. Settle into a comfortable position and close your eyes.

2. Become aware of your breath.

3. Notice and feel your breath as it goes in and out through your nose and mouth.

4. Now, shift your attention to inside your body, and notice what you are feeling.

5. Simply notice how you are feeling right now.

6. Notice if you are able to stay with this feeling and let it be, or if it is uncomfortable for you to stay with the feeling, just notice.

7. Now, breathe to the feeling, wherever it is in your body.

8. Focus your breath on the area of your body where the feeling is and imagine your breath going to the feeling.

9. Stay with your breathing as long as you feel comfortable.

10. When you feel ready, gently open your eyes.

As you experienced in this exercise, your breath brings your attention into your body and for a few moments out of your thinking mind—the conditioning. As you focus your breathing on the feelings within, you are re-connecting with your inner guidance: your feelings, your wants, and your needs.

I Don't Know What I Want

We live within our conditioned reality and make choices that are determined by our conditioning. We may be going along feeling satisfied. Sooner or later we find ourselves bored, disappointed, and feeling trapped within the choices we have made.

Marilyn, a 29-year-old woman, came to see me because a friend recommended she do so. She was unable to focus on her job and said that she often finds herself daydreaming at work just as she used to do in college. Marilyn was raised in a small

89

Midwestern town. Her father was a dairy farmer and her mother was a teacher. In high school, Marilyn was a good student. Her mother always told her that a college education was very important, and that it would provide her with security. Marilyn went to junior college for two years, and transferred to a state college where she continued to be a good student. She never became passionate about any particular major. On leaving college, Marilyn was unsure what type of job to apply for, and while shopping in a department store one day she saw that they were hiring for management positions and filled out an application. She met the requirement of having a college education and was subsequently hired.

Marilyn entered the management training program, and found the job was not what she really wanted to do, but she continued with the program because she had been accepted. When she finished the training program she was made assistant manager of woman's apparel. She spent the next five years in this position, even though she found it to be very boring. She was aware that she was not being promoted, and she believed that it is because she was not passionate about the job. Marilyn rationalized that she should not quit and look for another job, because she was making a decent living and it was allowing her to maintain her own apartment. Every day she found herself fantasizing and daydreaming when she was at work, and then she was not motivated to go out at night with friends. She further rationalized that her daydreaming and lack of motivation stemmed from how hard she worked. Marilyn told one of her friends that she was feeling trapped, and her friend suggested that she see a therapist and gave her my number.

Marilyn presented herself as an attractive, bright young woman with a lack of motivation. Her family history and conditioning reflected the values of two hardworking parents who were committed to the work they did and never entertained the possibility of changing their work. Marilyn never experienced her parents complaining about what they did, or discussing what they might have wanted to do more, or experiencing ambivalence.

Marilyn identified with her conditioning and was attempting to live within the conditioned identification of being a hardworking woman who was committed to her work and had no complaints. Marilyn's way of dealing with her boredom was through mentally escaping and not focusing on other life goals. Unlike Sam, she was not gratified by meeting the needs of her conditioned identification. Sam enjoyed the experience of plumbing and the knowledge that he was doing a good job, whereas Marilyn did not enjoy her work and merely sought to escape her experience at work through fantasy and daydreaming. When looking into the mirror of her soul, Marilyn acknowledged she was not living the life she wanted to be living. This was a very good first step in self-awareness.

Like Marilyn, many of us plod along without being passionate about our work, rationalizing the need to continue in the job with the thought that someday we will retire. Marilyn wanted to discover what was holding her back from taking charge of her life. She was unaware that her life was being lived as an extension of her conditioning. As she began to confront the conditioned identifications that led to her choice to remain in a job where she felt trapped, she was eventually able to make conscious choices that were more in alignment with her true self, which was beginning to emerge.

SNAP OUT OF IT NOW! MOMENT

Open Your Heart: Create Your Vision for Life

I am going to ask you to spend some time visualizing what you want for yourself, and to allow your heart to speak clearly to you of the vision you have for life. But first, I want you to treat yourself to a special place. Think of a place where you feel joy-filled, imaginative, and open to possibilities. It may be a place in nature or a special little nook in your own home. I love to sit on my upper balcony where I have a view of the mountains that surround Reno, and when I'm in San Diego, I love to sit on the sandstone rocks at my favorite beach, Windansea.

1. When you have settled into your special place, make yourself really comfortable.

2. Become aware of your breathing.

3. Feel as your breathing comes to a calm natural rhythm.

4. Close your eyes and say aloud to yourself: *If I can imagine it—it can be!*

5. Now ask yourself, *What do I want in life?*

6. Allow yourself the time for a clear vision to come into your imagination. Your vision for your life!

7. As it appears, become aware of the scope of your vision and all that it entails.

8. Attend to it with all your senses:

   - What do you see?

   - What do you smell?

   - How does your body feel, physically and emotionally?

   - Are there tastes associated with your vision?

   - What sounds are present within your vision?

9. Stay with this vision for as long as you like, focusing with all your senses.

10. When you feel ready, come back to the present and open your eyes.

Now, take out your journal and begin describing your vision for your life. As you journal be as specific as you can; identify all the aspects of this vision that you feel are significant. Write without censoring. Write until you feel you want to stop.

What comes next is up to you—that is, the timing of when you do it is up to you. I'm going to ask you to write a clear, concise, and specific vision statement for your life. You may want to take a break now and allow some space between your stream of consciousness writing and creating your vision statement. You decide what feels best for you. When you are ready to create your vision statement, you will use your journaling as the source for this vision. Create one or two sentences—no more than two—that describe your vision for your life clearly and specifically.

I WANT TO PLAY IN THE BIG LEAGUES

Most of us are told we have a special talent, and we want to succeed in a career using this talent. If we fail, we do not understand the reasons for our failure and we look for numerous rationalizations to make ourselves feel better. We never feel better, and go on wondering why we didn't make it. Every day, some young would-be star with great athletic talent fails to make it because of insufficient conditioning in one or more areas of life. They all want to be the next Tiger Woods, or Roger Federer, or Annika Sorenstam, but they are held back by their conditioning.

One client, Ted, entered my office and stated, "I am only going to be here one session, because I promised my girlfriend I would."

"Why did your girlfriend want you to see me?" I asked.

"She feels that I am defeating myself in my desire to become a major league baseball player. I am now playing at the level just one step below the Major Leagues, 'The Big Show,' and I have been there for five years. I have seen other players go from my team to the big leagues, and I think I'm at least as good as them. She is getting fed up with my frustrations, and I have to admit that I have been feeling angry a lot and I guess I take it out mostly on her. Also, my manager told me that if I don't get it together I am going back down.

"Ever since I was young I wanted to be a baseball player, and I have always felt I have a natural talent. I did very well playing ball in school, and instead of going to college I took a small bonus and played minor league ball. I was able to advance pretty quickly, and everyone told me that I have what takes to play in the majors. This is all I have ever wanted. My batting coach feels I should change my hitting stance so I can raise my average, but I hit naturally this way and I feel that I shouldn't change it. He also says that I need to work out more so I will be stronger and quicker. I feel comfortable with my strength and my quickness, and I think if I work out more it will change the way I feel. I have been told that I don't listen to my coach and manager, and that I think that I know better than them. I do listen to them and I really don't think I know better, but I do think I know myself better than they know me. They have been really great. I know they want me to succeed."

Since I only had one session with Ted, I explained to him that we are conditioned, we identify with our conditioning, and our conditioned identifications determine how we move through life. I said to him, "Ted, you are playing baseball within the conditioned identification: *My natural talent is all I need to get me to the Big Leagues.* You are creating a box that you cannot get out of, and you cannot see beyond the walls of this conditioned identification. Until you can break out of this box, you will be unable to accept the possibility of developing your natural talent with suggestions from other professionals, and potentially improving your game. If you think this makes any sense, I will be available to work with you. Let me know." In two weeks Ted called back and said he wanted to work with me.

The focus of our work together was to provide him with the tools he needed to learn to snap out of his conditioned identification that his natural talent was all he needed, and to de-condition his reaction, which he identified as resisting the suggestions from coaches to incorporate learned processes with his natural talent. He accepted that something wasn't working, or he would be in the Big Leagues. Ted was unaware of how negative his thinking and reacting had become. As he woke up to how he was interacting with his coaches, he made the decision that he would do whatever it took to achieve his goal. This included de-conditioning his resistance to developing his natural talent by altering the mechanics of his game, beginning strength and flexibility training, and working with a batting coach. After that, it didn't take Ted long to get into the Major Leagues.

Are you playing the game of your life fully and with zest? So many of us spend too much of our life over-thinking: a process that keeps us in a state of being disconnected from ourselves and disconnected from our ability to manifest what we want.

SNAP OUT OF IT NOW! MOMENT

Authentic Self, Authentic Power

Recognize and accept that with help—coaching, mentoring, counseling—you can develop your natural talent and learn to excel. The key is not to over-think your actions: trust your ability, connect with yourself, and be present. Stop thinking about how to excel, and go directly to excelling!

---

1. Identify what is holding you back. We now know it is your conditioned identification and the way you react to it, but you must identify: The specific belief, judgment, or expectation that is holding you back, and the reaction to this thought that is keeping you stuck in this belief.

2. Acknowledge you already have within you what it takes to excel. If you are feeling insecure about how to proceed—breathe away the insecurity and re-connect with yourself in this moment. Later, you will have the opportunity to work with what was provoking the insecurity—this is not the time.

3. Breathe away the negative resistance—negative thoughts and feelings—within you.

4. Re-connect with your authentic power and experience your excellence.

There is no magic to excelling, but there is a secret. Get out of your head. Stop thinking about past or future concerns, and get into the present moment where you are connected with your authentic power.

CHEMISTRY VS. CONDITIONING

We've all had the experience of meeting someone and immediately feeling drawn to them. You might say you have chemistry, or that you are soul mates. We connect on a level that is different and more satisfying than many of our other relationships, and we feel that we can say anything to this person and they will resonate to what we are saying and meet us with the same energy and enthusiasm. What is really going on? Why are we drawn to some individuals and avoid—or resist—getting to know others?

When we meet someone with similar conditioned identifications, we feel instantly understood, which is incredibly attractive. I recently introduced two friends of mine whom I knew shared similar upbringings and values. Both are 50-ish and living alone, both are immigrants who moved away from their families in adulthood and now live in the mountains of the United States, both receive their greatest joy while walking on nature trails, and they have similar features and even look similar. Afterward, each one of them have thanked me and said how rare it is to meet someone with whom the chemistry is so good. They each shared with me their feeling that fate has brought them together through me. This is a perfect example to illuminate how our conditioned identifications determine with whom we find attractive and how we relate.

I was talking with my mother the other day, and she shared her excitement in being asked to join a group in her church that had the goal of developing and promoting a sense of community within her local parish. She said that she likes the woman who is forming the group, and was pleased when this woman told her that the image of my mother's face was the first one that came to mind when thinking about putting the group together. My mother called to share how the first meeting went, and she told me how much she liked each woman in the group, especially the one who was closer to my mother's age. She shared a particular experience of connecting with this woman as an example of why she feels that they might develop a satisfying relationship with one another. As the women talked and joked with one another, this person looked at my mother and gave her a shove in the arm while she jokingly commented on the group's conversation. Chemistry struck! My mother tells me, "Here is someone of my generation! I like the way she shoved me, because I know I do this myself." She went on to share how when she has shoved me, one of my siblings, or one of her grandchildren in the arm while laughing about something between us we have responded with, "Ow, that hurts." She said, "The shove in the arm must be a gesture common to my generation and it feels good to be with someone else who uses it with me." We all seek to be heard, understood, and acknowledged, and with someone who perceives the world in a similar way, relating is easier.

Our relationships are determined by our conditioned identifications. We form friendships with others around our similarities in how we react to the same situation, because we have similar conditioned identifications surrounding this situation. We enter relationships with the same types of friends and we fall in love with similar kinds of mates. We often ask ourselves, *Why do I always fall for the same kind of man?* or *Why do the women I date always want the same thing?"* Why do we continue to get into the same type of relationships? It is because we are conditioned, and form conditioned identifications that keep us in our little box of relating. We say to ourselves, *I'll move to California and find someone new, and then I will be different.* Or we say, *I'll go on a cruise, buy new clothes that are different than I usually wear, and I'll meet new and exciting people.* Or, *I'll learn to scuba dive and be more adventurous and meet someone who is different from anyone I've ever met.* We are hoping that in this new environment we will be a clean slate, and we will suddenly be capable of experiencing ourselves differently. We count on the new environment, the new people, and the different experiences to change what it is that we don't like about the way we have been living our lives, and hope that this will take us out of our little box.

Until we wake up to our conditioned state of mind, and break free from the power of an unconscious conditioned identification, no matter where we go the conditioning will continue to determine the man or woman we fall for, how we think about ourselves, the way we interact with others, and the way we react to situations. The really good news, however, is that we always have the power to change our experience—to bring peace, beauty, and joy back into our life—and this power exists with awareness of the breath. Life is driven by the breath, whose control and development is one of my secret tools to resolving resistant negative conditioning.

SNAP OUT OF IT NOW! MOMENT

Open to the Mystery of Life that Surrounds You

We cannot define the mystery: infinity, the exquisite order of the Universe, and the meaning of life. We can identify the conditioned identifications that stop us from seeing the beauty of life and in ourselves. In defining negative conditioning we open ourselves up to feeling positive and finding positive solutions for our everyday challenges. In doing so, we are experiencing the mystery of life that surrounds us.

1. Take a walk with all your senses: out in a garden, along a hiking path, or simply in your backyard.

2. Be receptive to all that you encounter: the touch of air on your skin, the fragrance and tastes you pick up, the beauty of nature itself, the complex and simple textures, the sounds of nature.

3. Acknowledge your thinking. Be compassionate with yourself, the thinker.

4. Sense your breath and allow it to bring you back to the moment.

5. When you are thinking, you are not sensing. And, when you are sensing, you are not thinking.

6. With awareness of yourself breathing, you become aware of yourself in this moment. You are opening to the mystery of life that surrounds you.

CHAPTER SEVEN

Conditioned Reactions—The Tangible Reinforcement of Our Conditioned Reality

W e want to be capable of acting with choice. We can *see* that there are different ways to react to people and situations, but why do we keep reacting in the same way? This is our conditioned reality. Without knowing how to stop our reactions, we react in the same way over and over again—reinforcing our conditioning.

Our reactions to other people, to events, and even to our own thoughts are rooted in the conditioning that characterizes our development. We react according to how we've been conditioned, and whether or not this way of reacting continues to feel congruent and benefit our emerging authenticity, we go on reacting automatically and unconsciously. This is the way of the world.

The problem is, we never get what we want! Our conditioned reactions leave us feeling disconnected from the deeper part of ourselves and others.

So, what if:

- We want more?

- We want to react differently?

- We want to genuinely connect with one another?

- We want to stop the negative voices in our head?

- We want the freedom to act and react according to inner guidance rather then external rules?

- We want to live with purpose, joy, and excellence?

I believe the next evolutionary step for all of us as human beings is to wake up and break free from the walls of the conditioning: to consciously choose more! Snap Out of It Now! is an everyperson's guide to self-awareness, a truer connection with others, and a fuller experience of life. It is with awareness of your conditioned reactions that you have the opportunity to break free from your conditioned reality.

Many people believe they can control their reactions with sheer willpower. As you now understand from reading chapters 5 and 6, your rational thinking must take your conditioning into account, since you react not only to the situation at hand, but also to your internal conditioning, which is how you interpret and understand the situation. Once you shed light upon your own conditioning—the voices in your head representing thoughts that have become beliefs that have become the truths of your conditioned reality—you have the ability to choose your reactions. You can continue reacting according to your conditioning, or allow your next action to arise out of an authentic connection with yourself. Others, until they begin to confront their conditioning, will continue to react as they have been conditioned, but you will have the power to change. Your awareness of your conditioned reactions gives you the power to steer yourself in the right direction.

Here are some examples of automatic reactions that we engage without awareness:

- Your boss asks you to write a report on an event you attended. After you agree to do so, your body begins to feel tense. Immediately, your thinking becomes negative, and voices of doubt fill your head. You are reacting to this new work assignment by engaging negative and doubtful self-talk.

- You get a call that upsets you. Your mind tape gets stuck in negativity. As the tape goes on and on, feelings of frustration and anger find you finishing off a bag of cookies or chips.

- When a grandmother is asked if she will take care of her grandchild for a few hours, she may agree, thinking that she is being kind. The conditioned reality may be that she is really doing it because her conditioning is that grandparents take care of their grandchildren when

Reactions, in this context, are the behavioral expressions provoked by the feeling sensations that arise within our body. The feeling within the body arises naturally and then we condition ourselves to react: through passively denying or suppressing the inner feeling; through actively reacting toward a situation or person that we unconsciously associate with the underlying feeling; or through actively reacting toward ourselves by engaging in negative self-talk. Through our reaction we are disconnecting from our inner feelings, from conscious awareness of ourselves in the moment, and thus we are unable to break free from the walls of our conditioning.

asked. What follows is that she may feel irritated and put upon because it is inconvenient, and she did not really agree from choice, but reacted automatically according to her conditioning.

- When someone we care about asks us to tell them our truthful opinion about a purchase they have made, and we really don't think the article is attractive, we may believe we are choosing not to hurt their feelings. Really, though, we are reacting to our own conditioning to keep harmony, or to be liked by everyone, by being agreeable and saying, "That looks great."

- You are driving home after a bad day at work, and you tell yourself, *I won't get into another argument with my partner tonight.* You walk through the door, and regardless of your good intentions, something is said to throw you into a conflict. And, there you are, right where you said you would not be.

We are conditioned to be accommodating, kind, empathetic, and compassionate. To ignore, be insensitive to, jealous of, or avoid the verbal and nonverbal messages we receive from others also results from our conditioning. It is our conditioning to feel resentful of others when we perceive them as too needy; it is our conditioning that results in our confusion as to how—and whether or not—to respond to others. Our conditioning is also responsible for whether we eat a whole bag of chips when we feel frustrated or anxious, or whether we go for a long walk. What or who we wish ourselves to be, and who we imagine ourselves as being, is rarely consistent with the conditioning that has determined "who we are," and which continues to determine how we react.

Earlier in this book, I shared how unaware I had been of my own inner feelings of anxiety, fear, jealousy, sadness, and that these feelings were unconsciously triggering emotional reactions. In order to have control over our reactions, in order to consciously choose our actions, we must be willing to connect with the feelings within our body, which many of us have been conditioned to avoid. Conditioned avoidance does not offer any way of connecting with our inner feelings, owning them and working with them. The process of connecting with our inner feelings will allow us to connect with ourselves and face who we really are. From here, we are capable of choosing actions that are congruent with who we want to be!

Learning to control your reactions—arguing, intimidation, negative self-talk, or other unwanted behaviors—will allow you to master the situation.

Learning how to connect with your inner feelings that trigger your unwanted reactions—fear, from which all other negative feelings stem—will allow you to connect with your authentic power in the present moment and become the master of yourself!

Later in this book, you will learn the process of de-conditioning a conditioned reaction step by step. But first, let's practice a simple breathing awareness exercise that will guide you in connecting with your inner feelings—and thus, breaking the cycles of frustration, resentment, and anger that are so common in our human experience so we can continue smoothly on our path to self-awareness and positive conditioning.

SNAP OUT OF IT NOW! MOMENT

Connecting with and Releasing Inner Feelings of Frustration, Resentment, or Anger

Please make sure you have a quiet and comfortable space in which to practice the following exercise. You will learn how to recognize and acknowledge difficult emotions and transform them into a natural healing experience.

1. Settle into a comfortable position and close your eyes.

2. Allow your breathing to be whatever you feel at this moment.

3. When you have a rhythm that feels right for this time, begin to focus your breath on its passage in and out your nose, or if this is difficult use your mouth.

4. Your conditioned thinking will break your attention and you will loose focus.

5. Shift your attention back to the breath and refocus on your breath and your breathing.

6. Before you can release a negative emotion you have to connect with it—acknowledge and experience it within your body:

   • Where is it in your body?

   • In your tummy, chest, solar plexus, head, neck, throat?

   • What does it feel like? Perhaps it feels like warmth, tingling, tightness, hollowness, tension, coldness?

7. To do this, think of a situation in which you felt frustrated, resentful or angry. Perhaps it was an argument with a parent, friend, sibling, child, or spouse. Maybe a situation at work, or while driving in traffic.

8. Become fully aware of the emotions this memory triggers.

9. Focus on this sensation. Connect with your inner feeling using your breath.

10. Conditioned thoughts will break your focus. Simply re-focus on the emotion itself without the story behind it.

11. Now, breathe to the physical sensation of this feeling.

12. Focus your breath on the area of your body where this sensation is.

13. Imagine your breath going to the sensation.

14. As you breathe to the area of your body, experience the feeling.

15. If this is uncomfortable or difficult, don't try to change it. Just acknowledge the discomfort or difficulty. This will become easier with practice.

16. As you breathe to the feeling in your body, you are connecting with the feeling.

17. Your breath will release the discomfort as you exhale. The feelings of frustration, resentment, or anger will dissipate as you connect with the wholeness of yourself—body, mind, and spirit—in this moment.

18. When you are ready, gently open your eyes.

As you connect with and experience your inner feelings, as you are guided to do in this exercise, the emotion will dissipate, and no longer lead automatically to your conditioned reaction. In connecting with and experiencing the emotion, you are cutting the cord to your conditioned reaction.

We don't usually breathe to positive feelings, and this is a powerful practice! If you breathe to a negative feeling—fear, anger, feeling overwhelmed—it often dissipates, but when you breathe to a positive feeling—love, kindness, joy—the feeling expands within your body. Breathing to positive feelings can help you feel more connected with your inner power. I always feel re-energized. Try it for yourself the next time you are feeling filled with joy:

> *Stop*—acknowledge the feeling of joy.
> *Look*—where does it arise within your body?
> *Listen*—how does it feel within your body?
> *Breathe* to the feeling—experience the feeling expand through-out your body.

As discussed in chapter 1, we are conditioned to be unaware, and there are times when our partner, our friend, our coworker, or our child confronts us with the irrationality or unreasonable nature of our reactions. We find our only reaction is to defend our behavior, saying, "I don't know what came over me," or "I couldn't have reacted that way, that's not me," or conversely, "I can't help it, that is just who I am." We may know within ourselves there is truth to their comments, and yet we don't know how to confront this truth and work with our reactions. We go on reacting the same way.

We can take a simple event and turn it into the most illogical catastrophe in three seconds flat. See if this rings any bells: you go to your local ATM machine to make a withdrawal. The machine denies your withdrawal due to insufficient funds. Your stomach drops and your mind immediately goes nuts: *I'm sick of this bank! I just made a deposit two days ago...there is no way I can be over-drawn! They are so incompetent here—just another opportunity to stick it to the consumer with another fee. I paid ten bills yesterday and every one will bounce. I have to pay a donation at the Little League banquet tonight, and they only take cash. They will think I'm some kind of lowlife if I can't pay. My kid will be rejected and ostracized. I've got to change banks, but who's got time for the has-sle?*

Your reaction is a conditioned reaction. An alternative conditioned reaction may be to assume that you were the problem, not the bank: *I screwed up the math again. I'm always overdrawn. I've been trying to be more careful, but it's hopeless. Why am I so incompetent?* Do you see how we default to our conditioned reaction?

SNAP OUT OF IT NOW! MOMENT

Belly Breathing

The first step in changing a conditioned behavior is acknowledging to yourself, *I want to change my behavior.* Next, learning to stop it, even just for a moment. The experience of respite from thinking and doing is an experience of awakening. Breathing is free and automatic. When we consciously breathe we can have our breath work for us, not only to help us control the way we react, but also to pave the way to greater self-awareness and mastery!

Here's a simple breathing technique that will teach you to interrupt and stop the chatter inside your head: the non-productive noise.

1. Relax your jaw and allow your tongue to gently touch the roof of your mouth. This is a great tool for you jaw clenchers out there.

2. Relax your belly. Let it be. Often our desire for a firm tummy may make it difficult at first to just let it fall naturally.

3. Now, bring awareness to your breathing. Lightly place a hand over your belly button.

4. Focus on your breathing. Inhale to the count of four. Feel your breath fill your lungs and feel your hand on your belly rise.

5. Slowly exhale so that it lasts six counts. Feel your breath being released from your body and feel the hand on your belly lower.

6. Pause briefly at the end of the exhalation.

7. Never tighten your belly in order to make your exhalation last longer. Keep it relaxed. Simply slow down your exhalations.

8. Breathe four times: four counts on the inhalation and six counts on the exhalation.

9. Imagine your breath filling all three lobes of your lungs, pressing your diaphragm down so that your belly rises. This visualization will help you to become a more effective belly-breather.

10. Begin breathing:

Inhale: 1...2...3...4, and exhale: 1...2...3...4...5...6...pause...

Inhale: 1...2...3...4, and exhale: 1...2...3...4...5...6...pause...

Inhale: 1...2...3...4, and exhale: 1...2...3...4...5...6...pause...

Inhale: 1...2...3...4, and exhale: 1...2...3...4...5...6...pause...

Did you notice that, just for a moment, your mind was quiet? That just for a minute, the chatter in your head slowed down or stopped—and you did not react automatically? This simple technique will never fail you. It is something you can use in practical situations where it would not be appropriate to leave the situation, like discussions at work, with your partner, children, or any time you find yourself engaging an automatic negative reaction—whether it is internal negative self-talk or external blame—and therefore disconnected from what is actually happening in the present moment.

Our reactions are conditioned, so how does one get consensus with regard to what reactions and behaviors are appropriate and reasonable?

Let's wake up! Only you can decide whether your reaction is appropriate or reasonable. Within the conditioning, the consensus will come from others who exist within similar conditioned realities. However, if you are on the path to your authentic power—to becoming your own conditioner—you will be able to discern, through the experience of the feelings within your body, how you will respond to any situation, event or person. Awareness of your conditioned reaction gives you the power to connect with your inner guidance and, with the power of breathing awareness, the freedom to choose your next action.

Within your relationships with your loved ones, and even within your relationships with your coworkers, you may have tried establishing agreements with one another in order to communicate and relate more effectively. At work, for example, you may have needed to set up an agreement with your secretary that should he need to leave early on any given day, he will leave a note on his desk of his day's to-do list with the items unattended to highlighted. At home, your partner may have promised you not to drink alcohol on weeknights. You may even have a third party—a counselor, therapist, or trusted friend or colleague—participate in order to lend clarity and reason to the agreement you were attempting to establish. Predictably, your secretary or partner will end up breaking the agreement as they return to their so-called unreasonable, conditioned reactions and behaviors. Until your partner, secretary, child, toll-booth operator, and mother-in-law confront their own conditioning, acknowledge and accept the inappropriateness of the reaction, and then make the commitment to decondition the reaction, they will be unable to react differently.

We cannot change our negative reactions without facing that we are conditioned to react this way. Be clear with yourself: *I am conditioned and the other person is conditioned; I will react my way and the other person will react their way.* When you are presented with a way out of your seemingly endless conflicts with another person, acknowledging your conditioning and the fact of the other's conditioning can avoid future fights from breaking out.

Anger is a potent example of a conditioned reaction. In the first place, it explodes automatically before we are cognitively able to acknowledge the situation. Secondly, we have no awareness of the feeling within our body that is provoking the impulse to react outwardly, and as we are unable to resolve the anger, we end up repeating the same angry reactions from one situation to another. The only good news is in regard to self-awareness: we can almost always see and feel the consequences of our angry reactions. The reaction of anger is a common, and potentially aggressive and destructive reaction, in which many of us engage. I have chosen to focus on the conditioned reaction of anger in the following examples.

The anger we feel originates within us and is provoked by our conditioned identifications even though it may feel like the actions of another/others caused our feeling.

A client of mine, Phyllis, experiences anger when she perceives that her son's wife has disrespected her; this anger leads to conflicts at family events. What Phyllis is beginning to realize is that both she and her daughter-in-law may have different definitions for what it means to disrespect someone. Phyllis feels disrespected when her calls to her son's home are ignored. Her perception is that her daughter-in-law sees the caller ID and just doesn't answer. Phyllis has begun to accept that this perception and her reaction to it is her conditioning, and that whether or not it reflects the accurate motives of her daughter-in-law is really irrelevant. In taking charge of her life and her experience of self, Phyllis is learning how to breathe away the feelings of anger and choose to attend family events with feelings of love.

Skewed perceptions and identification with our conditioning can lead to aggressive negative thought patterns, and even negative aggressive actions. We know that uncontrolled anger can lead to tragic situations, but most of us are unaware of how powerful our conditioned identifications and their reactions are in leading to an inability to control the angry reactions.

An example of this was seen in a news report of several years ago: the father of a soccer player beat his son's coach to death. This story has always stuck with me, as it so clearly illustrates how unconscious one can become once they enter a cycle of conditioned reactions. At all competitive events we may hear someone say, "Kill the umpire," or "Kill the coach," but rarely does this ever occur. I remember there was much discussion around this incident as many people were able to identify with the feelings provoked when they see a loved one treated badly. We might try to understand the good intention gone wrong; it was reported that the father watched the coach bully his son, and then simply intended to defend his son. We might even see this incident as the natural response of a father wanting to protect his son and then losing control. In this incident, the father's conditioned need to protect his son provoked anger, which in turn triggered an aggressive action. Once the father began the cycle of conditioned reactions he lost conscious awareness of himself, as well as any ability to exert control over his reactions. Within our conditioned reality, we can be capable of actions that may be contradictory to our emerging authenticity. Cycling, which we will discuss in chapter 8 ("Cycling within Our Conditioned Reality"), leads one into a state of being identified with the reaction. We may identify ourselves as an angry person—or as pure anger—and thus become unable to hear any rational prohibitions or look at the consequences of our reactions.

We say a behavior is natural or instinctive when the behavior occurs without our thinking mind directing it. The conditioned identifications and conditioned reactions that assume control of our lives feel natural. For example, the media has given focus to the issue of whether or not Pete Rose should be allowed into the Hall of Fame as a result of his gambling and his dishonesty with regard to these behaviors. Mr. Rose acknowledged his gambling in his book, *My Prison Without Bars:* "I'm sure I'm supposed to act all sorry or sad or guilty now that I've accepted that I've done something wrong. But you see, I'm just not built that way." Here is a case where a person has not been conditioned to react with regret, sadness, or guilt. His behavior and dialogue both exhibit a lack of awareness of himself and his conditioning.

Clients have often asked me, "What is the difference between a conditioned reaction and an instinctual reaction?" An instinctual reaction is hardwired into the brain. For example, a child will pull his or her finger away when they touch a hot stove. Yet, when we say that we react instinctively with anger when someone pushes us or steps on our toe, that is our conditioning. We have been conditioned to defend ourselves, and anger is the reaction which sets up the action of defending ourselves. The instinctual reaction would be to step back or pull our toe away. The conditioned reaction is to push the person back, or to step on their toe in retaliation.

You might ask about the fight or flight reaction that has been passed down through evolution. This response is an internal reaction, and the reaction takes place on a biochemical level. How we process this internal reaction, and then how we in turn react externally, depends upon our conditioning.

We attempt to control our reactions through statements, such as *Think before you act*, and then believe that this will allow us to put a gap between the experience and the engagement of the reaction. What we are not conditioned to do is experience ourselves reacting—to notice the feeling that arises in the body, and then observe how we react to the feeling. Our conditioning is simply to react. It is in experiencing ourselves reacting that we become self-aware and thus capable of controlling our reaction—by not engaging it, or by delaying it.

We can stay with the feeling of anger, breathe into the sensation in the body, and then choose to react with patience or compassion for ourselves and for the other. This ability to stop the reaction does not mean that we deny the anger within us: it means just the opposite. It is the unconscious engagement with our conditioned reaction that allows us to deny the anger within us. As we use awareness of our breath to connect with the feeling of anger, we empower ourselves with the ability to stop the outward aggressive reaction. Anger is a natural human experience. It is our conditioning that has turned it into something that is acted out rather than felt and experienced.

With awareness of our conditioned identifications, the practice of de-conditioning, and the experience of choice with regard to our engagement with the conditioned reactions, we have the opportunity to become a participant in our own conditioning.

SNAP OUT OF IT NOW! MOMENT

Break Free from Your Unwanted Reaction

When you are in a situation that you have recognized provokes a negative conditioned reaction, such as blaming or doubting yourself or others, yelling, complaining, or engaging in an unwanted behavior, you can consciously acknowledge the situation and act accordingly. Here, I've broken down steps to help you through these situations as you learn how to pause the reaction and feel capable of choosing how you will respond.

1. Recognize the conditioned identification that is getting you down. Maybe you were supposed to perform better in an interview, get a better grade on an exam, bake better

cookies for a party, make more money on a deal, finish a project more quickly.

Now, write out the specific content of the thought, belief, or voice in your head:

_____

_____

_____

_____

2. Identify the way this thought, belief, or voice makes you feel:

    _____

    _____

    _____

    _____

3. Focus your breathing on the area of your body where the feeling arises, and simply breathe to this area. Experience your feeling.

4. Accept that you are disappointed, upset, sad, or whatever the emotion might be for you. You have a right to feel whatever arises within you; this is a natural human experience. Don't deny yourself this privilege.

5. Experience the reaction you would normally have. Many of them boil down to, *You're a failure, because someone else says so,* followed by negative self-talk and self-degradation.

6. If you are able to take a break, give yourself a specified amount of time to journal. Bring to awareness, through writing, your experience of how you typically react to this conditioned identification. What is your personal awareness of this situation? What do you do, say, and think? If

you're in the middle of a situation and unable to break away, treat this situation as training and practice. Become aware of how you are reacting in the moment. How do you act or interact? What do you say? What are you thinking? Observe and witness yourself reacting even while in the middle of your reaction. Later you will have the opportunity to write about this experience, cry, meditate, go running, or take a hot bath—and congratulate yourself on increasing self-awareness.

7. Plot your course of action. You may want to apologize if the way you normally react is negative toward the other person(s). Now, choose to act in a way that is most beneficial and positive to you, even if it feels uncomfortable or wrong due to your conditioning. This might mean:

   a. Apologizing for your reaction to someone who has insulted you, instead of remaining angry and self-righteous.

   b. Doing another presentation, if your team at work didn't approve of the first one, instead of defending it and creating a stressful work environment.

   c. Trying a new diet plan if the current one has caused you to gain weight, instead of turning to Ben and Jerry's to soothe your sorrow.

Whatever your conditioned reaction is, if it were good for you, you wouldn't be questioning it. Initially, this new behavior will not feel good, but keep in mind that in acting this way you are taking care of yourself; you are breaking free from the control of your reaction.

In this process, as with all processes within this book, feel free to turn to your journal, your friends or to this book for support. I believe in you! You wouldn't be reading this book

> if you were not ready to wake up and take charge of your life now!

Your conditioning tells you to avoid the feelings in your body by going ahead and engaging a negative reaction. As you engage your conditioned reaction, you may feel emotionally comfortable. The reaction has effectively distanced us from the difficult feeling within. If you have decided that your conditioned reaction isn't working for you, then take charge of your life, connect with your authentic power, and choose an action that you know will affect your life positively.

CHAPTER EIGHT

Cycling within Our
Conditioned Reality

Each day we start out wanting the day to be different from any we have ever had—and then we find this day to be the same as every other day. We react to the same thoughts in our head; we react to the same behavior in our partner, our friend, our boss, and even in strangers. Our lives fall into routine circular patterns—we *try the same things and expect different results*. We want to move forward with our lives but the circular logic, or *cycling*, that is part of our conditioned reality is holding us hostage.

Our lives are full of cycles. The cycles of the moon, the seasons, sleep, and hunger—all things come in cycles. Life cycles allow us to live without giving thought to life's little details, so we can focus on accomplishing our goals. On average, 90 percent of mental processing is unconscious, and about 95 percent of behavior is the result of a conditioned life cycle.[1] People do things because they learned to do them in a certain way, and rarely consider

---

1. Brian E. Walsh, PhD. *Unleashing Your Brilliance*. Victoria, Canada: Walsh Seminars, 2005.

whether or not these ways of interacting continue to be helpful and life-enhancing. We just continue within the program of our lives. As we wake up to our conditioned awareness, we discover the power to stop negative life cycles and enhance positive life cycles.

Think of driving to work in the morning. You know the route and follow it effortlessly while you plan your workday. You know where to exit without reading the signs. Following the correct route is conditioned, just a cycle in your daily routine.

Say one day you are going to the dentist—something different from your daily routine—but as soon as you hit the freeway your mind goes on autopilot. Your thoughts might be on your plans for the weekend or on an incident at home. The next thing you know, you are zipping past the exit you need to take to get to your destination. Suddenly, you're on your way to the office. This happens to us all. We engage a life cycle without realizing it, interrupting our plans and taking us in the wrong direction. Taking the wrong road by taking the road often traveled is a typical example of how our cycling can take control of our life path without our awareness.

The unintended side-effect of a functional cycle is that this cycle takes us out of conscious awareness of ourselves. When we are in a cycle of unconscious repetition, whether it be to get us to work on time, complete our domestic chores or finish our workout routine, we are mindlessly, without conscious awareness, going through the steps we are conditioned to take. We are in a cycle of conditioned reactions.

After one of my Stress Relief through Meditation seminars, an attendee once asked, "When I drive to work sometimes I have no memory from the time I leave my home and when I arrive at work. Is that similar to meditation?"

He had an excellent question, whose answer clarifies the intention of meditation. In fact, these two experiences, meditation and cycling, are diametrically opposed. With meditation, one focuses his or her attention on being in the present moment. Within the experience of cycling, such as the cycling that gets us to work on time, one focuses on the past or the future. Meditation is about increasing our awareness of our experience; cycling is about being pulled away from the experience of ourselves within the present moment, into a conditioned reality created by our conditioned thoughts, emotions, and behavioral reactions. Awareness takes intentional focus.

Now, don't get me wrong, I get it. As individuals, as a society, as a culture, we are all busy. There are 24 hours in a day and we feel that they need to be filled with activities: doing everything to the sun and moon and back, from everyday work and chores to walking the dog and meeting up for cocktails. We feel like there isn't enough time in the world for us, and every time we glance at the clock more minutes have slipped away. When you're feeling anxious or overwhelmed because of the time, you're mind is going into overdrive. An unconscious cycle of conditioned reactions has been activated. This is when you need to *stop, look,* and *listen:* breathe in awareness of yourself in the present moment and con- nect with your senses. Instead of speeding up into a hectic frenzy, take a nice, deep, relaxing breath and slow down a little. As you sense your breath going in and out through your nose and mouth, you are experiencing a moment of relief from your overactive thinking. You are breaking the cycle, and you are connecting with yourself, body, mind, and spirit. You will be surprised how much better you'll feel. You'll think more clearly and actually get more done.

No matter how hectic your day, you must find time—even if only a few minutes—to connect with yourself in the present moment; to find moments of self-nourishment in each day. I have learned to enjoy the process of doing the laundry, making the bed, as well as sitting peacefully on my balcony enjoying views of the mountains, as these are actions that, when I choose to do them mindfully, allow me to experience moments of freedom from my overactive, thinking mind. When you don't take time for self-nour- ishment, those dominant conditioned identifications that are not working for you will just keep blocking your progress. Why is it that we are so unwilling to nurture ourselves, but we don't do anything to stop poisoning our minds with negativity? As you remain disconnected from yourself within the conditioning, your negative reactions become so ingrained, so much a part of yourself, that you live within this cycle the rest of your life without ever being aware of what you are really doing—and always wondering, *Why do I keep ending up where I started?* It's not worth it to live your life totally in the fast lane. I am aware that the fast lane can be more efficient and effective at times, but without time to breathe and connect with what's real in your life—yourself and the people you love—you'll never enjoy the beauty in the world. In the end, you'll hold yourself back by trying to get ahead through haste.

SNAP OUT OF IT NOW! MOMENT

Breather

If your tendency is to multitask—household chores, talking on the phone while checking email—acknowledge this tendency. Give yourself permission to connect with yourself in this moment; nothing is more important. Give yourself a break. Stop the cycle. Take a couple of minutes for a Snap Out of It Now! breather:

Stop what you are doing.

Look at your surroundings.

Listen to yourself breathing.

Experience a moment of relief from your thinking mind.

Now, decide what one thing you will focus on, and allow yourself the freedom to fully experience and enjoy this one thing: your to-do list, meditation, the laundry or dishes, time with your partner or child, or sitting in your favorite chair to relax. The reality is that there is "no such thing as multitasking! The brain only really attends in one sense at one time. By attempting to do more, you are actually diminishing the capability to attend to anything. What people consider good multi-tasking is actually effective and efficient 'shifting' of attention." (Louis Csoka, www.Apexperform.com)

WHAT IS A CYCLE OF CONDITIONED REACTIONS?

Cycles of conditioned reactions begin in an unconscious effort to reinforce the feeling within us that we are loved. We continue cycling with behaviors that we may later find are incongruent with our inner desires, in an unconscious effort to retain our bond with a significant other. Negative habits are reinforced again within this unconscious need to feel connected to those we love, despite ourselves. Subconsciously, we believe that if we stop cycling as we have been conditioned, our significant others will no longer love us.

We all have recurring thoughts. In fact, most thought is repetitive; up to 95 percent of everything we are thinking is following a pattern of already established thinking. When we have a thought that constantly recurs and causes the same action over and over, this is a cycle: a habitual pattern of thoughts and reactions. The thought process and subsequent reaction can be either positive or negative.

Once a cycle is activated, we automatically react to a voice in our head, or to our interpretation of an event or the behavior of another person, and this reaction triggers consecutive reactions that feed the cycle. It will run its course. Therefore, once we have entered a cycle of reactions, we have no conscious control over our reactions.

Within the cycle:

- We are not aware that we are reacting according to a program.

- We are not aware that we are conditioned to cycle.

- We are not aware that each time we engage a cycle we are strengthening the cycle of conditioned reactions; we are reinforcing our program.

- We are not aware of ourselves in this moment. Our full attention is within the story created by our conditioned reality.

We cycle with our conditioned thought processes and consequent actions and reactions, despite negative consequences. On one hand, perhaps your mother always warned you of the dangers of the sun's rays, and you internalized her concern for your skin. To protect yourself from health risks, you were conditioned to apply sunscreen before leaving the house each day. As a result you have healthy, glowing skin. On the other hand, maybe you were conditioned by your friends and advertisements to believe that smoking makes you feel like you're cool and you belong, and that to look cool you need to light a cigarette. Every time you go to a coffee shop or bar, you chain-smoke. You want to quit smoking, but you don't feel cool when you go out without a pack of cigarettes. Some patterns are a necessary and healthy part of your life, while others are worth changing.

On an *Oprah* show sometime ago I saw a group of female actors—Nicole Kidman, Meryl Streep, and Julianne Moore—discussing their tendency, after accepting a new role, to automatically think that no one will want to come to the theaters to watch them any more. Each of them said that after they accepted a role in a new film, they always wanted to call their agent a few days later to get them out of the commitment. When Meryl Streep shared that she would say to herself, *No one will want to see me. I'm too old*, Nicole Kidman quickly added, "I can't believe that—I do the same thing!" Sitting there with Oprah, they were able to laugh at themselves as they revealed their own specific self-disparaging judgments. Obviously, these women are aware of their conditioned identifications, while finding a way to de-condition their reaction to reject the role so they are able to accept the job and give a remarkable performance. Having the capacity to laugh at oneself is a tremendous asset in working with conditioning.

EXPOSING CONDITIONED CYCLES

When I was in graduate school I used to berate myself after exams, never realizing how much time I spent putting myself down and criticizing my intellectual ability. I was engaging in a cycle of insecurity and self-flagellation. The idea of someone evaluating my work and finding me inadequate provoked my conditioning to question myself, and I would react by doubting my intelligence and ability to complete the exam competently. It made no difference that I had scored well on previous exams.

When the next exam was taken, I would automatically enter this cycle of self-denigration. No matter how many reminders I received from a friend or my husband regarding my previous accomplishments, the completion of the exam would provoke my conditioning and I would enter the cycle. Not yet aware that I was reacting to my conditioned identification and that I was conditioned to react in this disparaging way, I became identified not only with the thought, *I have failed,* but also with the reaction: anxiety. In these moments, I believed myself to be inadequate and my reactions reflected my disappointment and anger at my own inadequacy. My engagement with this cycle resulted in my wasting the rest of the day in a downward spiral of negativity leading to self-pity.

Another example of cycling that works against us may be seen in the actions of a client, Stacy, in a business meeting with her new boss. She was aware that her boss typically leaves other coworkers in tears after an evaluation, and she was determined not to let this happen in her interactions with her boss. However, to her dismay she found herself unable to control her tears in a recent conflict with her boss. She shared her experience during a discussion: she immediately disagreed with her boss on a few issues, and wanted to share an idea that she felt would allow for improvement in the business. Before she knew it, she was sitting stiffly on the edge of her chair with one hand on her boss's desk, feeling irritated that she was unable to get a word in. Her irritation soon became anger as he interrupted every attempt she made to enter the conversation. As she sat there waiting for a moment to speak, she became increasingly anxious. When he finally stopped talking to allow her to say something, she burst into tears. Stacy said, "I could almost feel the cycle of emotions building, but I felt I had no control over the course of these emotional reactions." The meeting ended with her having to excuse herself with apologies.

Later, she felt humiliated and unresolved about the anger she felt toward her boss, and yet frightened of repeating her experience. Stacy was at a loss as to how to interrupt this emotional cycle and be capable of responding more professionally to the intimidating behavior her boss displayed. Many of us will find ourselves in similar cycles of conditioned reactions. Depending upon our conditioning, when faced with an aggressive or intimidating interaction with another, we may find ourselves lashing out and thus loosing respect; we may feel unable to respond to at all; or, we may end up, like Stacy, collapsing into tears. Regardless of the cycle, when it isn't working for you, you already possess the power to change it!

Once a cycle is activated, it will run its course. Our awareness is focused on the reality of our conditioned thoughts and judgments, on the righteousness or justifications for our actions, or it may be on the spiral of disturbing sensations and feelings experienced within our body. We might try to end the experience of ourselves cycling by diverting our attention to something else—working out, going shopping, or going to a movie. We may use food, alcohol, or chemical substances to change our experience from a downer to an upper, or in our hope to get rid of the feelings altogether, or we may become the victim and seek comfort within this conditioned reality. We are not aware that we are cycling within the reality of a conditioned identification, and we are not aware that we cannot stop the cycle at will.

In these moments, our conditioned awareness reflects our total identification with our conditioning: conditioned thoughts, beliefs, expectations, judgments, and ways of interacting. That is, we do not know that the particular conditioned identification that has been activated is our conditioned reality, because we simply experience it as our reality. Until we wake up to our conditioning and recognize that our thinking, and how we react to our thinking, has been programmed into us, we have no way of separating who we are from what we think and how we interact. And we are unable to manifest that which we truly want for ourselves: excellence!

Identify a Negative Cycle in Your Life

Stop, look, and *listen.* Wake up to your authentic power! Each one of you has the power to stop your negative life cycles, and to enhance and build upon your positive life cycles.

Take a moment in a quiet and comfortable space. You cannot be free from a conditioned cycle until you bring awareness to it. Bring to your awareness a negative cycle you would like to break free from.

1. Using the examples above of myself and my client Stacy, identify a negative cycle that is inhibiting you in some way. Describe the circumstances of the interaction: how do you react?

    _____

    _____

    _____

2. What is your conditioned belief that is dominant with this cycle?

    _____

    _____

    _____

3. How do you feel when you confront this belief? Take a moment with this question. Become aware of your breath and connect with yourself in this moment. Ask yourself, what is the inner feeling in response to your conditioned belief?

    _____

    _____

    _____

4. Recognize that your reaction is being provoked by this inner feeling.

5. Acknowledge and experience the feeling now. Notice where in your body this feeling is, and focus your breath there. As you breathe with awareness of the feeling, you are allowing yourself to experience the feeling without the distraction of your conditioned story that underlies the feeling.

6. What do you notice about your experience with the feeling sensation?

    _____

    _____

    _____

7. Spend some time with yourself and, if you feel ready, describe your present experience of self—body and mind.

_____

_____

_____

Either take some time for yourself to respond to these questions right here, or use your journal to explore your experience. This exercise is to help you start acknowledging your automatic reactions and recognize how the negative cycle begins. Be kind and compassionate with yourself: you are taking responsibility for your life! Allow yourself to be creative in your expression. Make a chart, draw a picture, or create lists. Don't feel you have to form full sentences! Do whatever it takes to stay in the flow of expression. You are awakening to your conditioned reality, and taking charge of your life by learning how to expose the cycles of reaction that no longer serve you.

Remember: every day is a blessing, and if you are taking the time to read this book in search for your authentic power, you are already in the top .01 percent of the most proactive people in our society. Since you have already made the resolution to make changes in your life and make the coming years better than ever before, you're one of the lucky ones! I am teaching you how to be your own personal life guide; to take possession of the inner joy you innately know is your birthright. My lessons are simple and profound. They will stay with you for the rest of your life. You will become your own conditioner and live life in congruence with your deeper nature.

Confrontation and acknowledgment of your conditioning—conditioned reactions and their cycles—leads to greater self-awareness. Once you confront your conditioning, which you will be doing in the next section of this book, you will understand that

We rarely acknowledge and allow ourselves to experience the inner feeling. This is because most of us are not conditioned to express our feelings—particularly feelings such as anger, disappointment, frustration, and impatience. Therefore, we don't know what to do with the feelings that arise within us, and in fact most of us are conditioned to avoid the feeling by engaging outward reactions. We know we want to stop the cycling that keeps us stuck feeling negatively about ourselves, and reacting so negatively toward others, but we don't know that in order to stop the cycle we have to literally cycle back to the feeling within our body that triggers the reaction.

like the memories in your photo album, the conditioned identifications will always be a part of you, but as you become consciously aware of yourself, you will break through the walls of the conditioning and be capable of re-conditioning yourself in a fresh, positive way, making your negative reactions nothing more than a memory of the past. In the third section of the book, you will learn the invaluable process of de-conditioning: the Snap Out of It Now! method.

You've already come a long way. Now it's time to live with awareness of your conditioning and manifest the life of your dreams.

CHAPTER NINE

Acknowledgment and Acceptance of Our Conditioning

W e acknowledge that our reality is conditioned. We come face to face with who we have been conditioned to be, recognizing that the ways in which we see ourselves—our thoughts, our judgments, our beliefs, our expectations, and our stories—dominate and determine the way we live our life, stopping us from living our dreams.

Despite our conditioning, our doubts and our skepticism, strength and capability are in all of us. You will find your inner power. Acknowledge your desire to break free of the destructive patterns caused by your conditioning. Confrontation with your conditioned identifications will lead to living and breathing with awareness, and finding your inner joy.

I coach individuals through a variety of negative identifications.

- Are you mired in a dysfunctional relationship because you are afraid to be alone?

- Do you know clearly what you want for yourself, but wonder why the fulfillment of your dream continues to elude you?

- Do you let fear or doubt overcome your ability to take action, even when you know the action you must take will help you achieve the goals you have set for yourself?

- Are you dreaming the life of a professional athlete rather than living your dream?

- Are you living a life you feel was constructed for you, rather than doing the things you had always hoped to be doing?

- Do you just feel dissatisfied, anxious or angry?

Every person's story is different, but also the same. People are all conditioned, and must face the problems engendered by their conditioning: self-doubt, unworthiness, anxiety, fear, panic or uncontrollable anger. Opening up your awareness by confronting your conditioning will enable you to take control of your destiny. This chapter is about acknowledging and accepting your conditioning and taking control of your life.

THE BLEARY EYED MONSTER: PROJECTILE EMOTING

In our efforts to avoid or to deny core conditioned identifications, we sometimes project onto others what we cannot—or refuse to— see in ourselves. Remember my experience with my husband that I described in the first few pages of this book? You can be like a camera, capturing a script of thoughts, feelings, and sensations as portrayed by other people in a film. You might not realize that the thoughts, feelings and sensations that you are seeing in others are those that you are experiencing within yourself. You are the projector, and also the images on the screen. When you do not realize you are projecting onto others, you may unconsciously act out violently, physically, verbally, or nonverbally. Before you lash out at any person—or, as you catch yourself lashing out at someone—*stop, look, listen* and *breathe* to your inner experience. Think about how you perceive the situation. Are you seeing behavior or emotions in this other person that you can also see within yourself? You may be projecting your own conditioned identifications onto the other person.

SNAP OUT OF IT NOW! MOMENT

Personal Time Out

Take a personal time out. You are entitled to experience compassion for yourself.

1. Acknowledge what behaviors and/or emotions you are seeing in another.

2. *Stop, look,* and *listen* within yourself. Are the same patterns within you?

3. Breathe with this new awareness.

Helpful Hint: Try to remember that what pleases or irritates you about others, as this reflects your satisfaction—or dissatisfaction—with the same thing in yourself. You cannot recognize what is not within yourself. The admirable and not-so-admirable attributes people notice in others are often their own attributes. In this way, we are who we say others are. As you recall the judgments, criticisms, and perceptions you make toward others, or those you find you have projected onto others, you can include them in your inventory; these are the judgments, criticisms, and perceptions—core conditioned identifications—you hold to yourself.

To be able to make positive changes in your life, it is important to be honest and forthright about who you are. The following 24 hours exercise is a good way to get in touch with who you are and what conditioned reactions you would like to change to better your life.

TAKE 24 HOURS

When we are aware of our conditioning, we will experience parts of ourselves that we deny and overlook. As we face our conditioned identity, we become more than we were conditioned to be. Awareness is the gateway to freedom.

Conditioned identifications are present in every moment of our life. I have chosen to take a 24-hour period to work with as a format to help illustrate how we can bring to awareness the conditioned identifications that we live with day in and day out. You, too, can take 24 hours to begin your inventory and start to catalogue your everyday thoughts, judgments, actions and reactions.

At any given point, if you are committed and thoroughly working this process, it is highly likely that you may feel lost and discouraged. Don't give up! You might need to pause—*stop, look,* and *listen* to what is bringing your reaction to the surface. Breathe. The good news is that you are getting closer to becoming aware of and identifying the conditioning that has been holding you back.

Now, after devoting years to writing and intensely confronting my own conditioned identity, I am aware of the core conditioned identifications that are provoked and which determine and impact the way I feel, act, and react, and I am aware the moment I engage a conditioned reaction. Sometimes I go ahead and enter the cycle of reactions and experience something akin to *déjà vu*, and other times I am able to stop the cycle by not reacting. I am aware of myself consciously taking on the role of core conditioner for myself.

I would like to share a section of my first 24 hour exercise. To show how our awareness of core conditioned identifications will emerge throughout our day, and how our conditioned reactions will often lead us to awareness of other conditioned identifications,

I have italicized the core conditioned identifications and conditioned reactions that emerged in the process of doing my 24 hour exercise. It is amazing when I compare those days to the person I am today.

My First 24 Hours

I wake up and look at the clock. It is 7:15 a.m. *I judge myself for not waking up earlier, and I think about all the people I know who are already up and actively engaging their work.*

I am lazy. I am not productive. My life is wasting away.

If I lay in bed longer, telling myself, that I deserve to enjoy lying in bed and allowing my body to awake according to its own timing, the negative judgments increase: *I am not working hard enough and therefore will never be successful; other people are already accomplishing so much more than me.* Battling these thoughts, the tension becomes unbearable. I try to counter these negative thoughts by rationalizing that I work very hard during the day and there really is no reason for me to jump out of bed at that moment. I try telling myself that my job is to confront my conditioning so that I can write clearly about this process—and this requires different work habits, not less productive work habits. This is a rationalization, as I am not actually confronting the conditioning, rather I'm simply telling myself that in order to relieve guilt provoked within the conditioning.

I go to the bathroom and brush my teeth. I look in the mirror and tell myself, *Cheer up. Don't be such a downer.* As I say this, I hear the echoes of my father's voice.

As I go into the kitchen to begin making breakfast, my husband, who has been working in his office, calls out an endearment and the sound of his voice brightens my spirits. I enjoy the process of putting breakfast on the table and enjoy greeting my husband for breakfast. At this time in the morning, my experience shifts and I feel a sense of excitement reflecting the fleeting thought, *This is a new day and the possibilities are endless. I can do anything I want.*

I think about writing today and I pray that I will be productive and accomplish a lot. I finish my meal much sooner than Barry, and begin to feel restless. *Time is flying by, and I still haven't accomplished anything.* I do my morning domestic chores while thinking about getting down to my office to begin writing. I think about my book, and I think about how nice it will be when it is published and acknowledged as a good book, and then I criticize myself for wishful thinking, and again telling myself, *I'm not working hard enough to really achieve success.* Then I tell myself, *I am following my path and the book I am writing will be helpful to many people.* This thought encourages me as I think, *I am working on my purpose in life.*

I practice awareness of breath before beginning my writing session. During the breathing many conditioned identifications arise, similar to the ones to do with my own productivity and desire for acknowledgment that arose upon awakening. I go back to the breathing. Afterwards, I go down to my office and turn on the computer. I start by checking my email messages, and succeed in avoiding writing (this is what I cynically tell myself) for that much longer. I begin to feel irritable, anxious, and angry, as I get closer to opening my book and writing. I feel overwhelmed at the idea of trying to convey all that needs to be conveyed for the book to make sense and be worthwhile to others. I begin to doubt that I have what it takes to write this book. I experience tension in my chest and awkwardness throughout my body. I doubt my ability to articulate my thoughts with creativity and intelligence. I experience fear and anxiety.

I must acknowledge these reactions—overwhelmed feelings, doubt, physical tension, fear, anxiety—as the conditioned reactions to my core conditioned identification: *I have no voice of worth; I will never be capable of writing all that I believe needs to be written in order to convey the concept of my book with clarity; I cannot do it alone; my words are inadequate and boring; I don't have anything to say; I am inadequate as a writer and a woman.* If I do not, I will cycle with them, which often turns into a problem (deciding to respond to an upsetting email, or getting into an argument with my husband over something irrelevant) and delays the onset of my writing session.

I sit down. I acknowledge the reactions, and then I breathe with the tension in my body as I begin the writing session. Throughout the session feelings of fear and doubt and anger arise as reactions to my core conditioned identifications: *I am not good enough; this sentence is crap; my writing is too simplistic; no one will understand what I am trying to say; I am worthless; I have to write it perfectly the first time.* If they go unacknowledged, I will react by micromanaging my writing; I will spend excessive amounts of time rewriting a particular example, and wasting more time.

With the acknowledgment, I am able to get into the process of writing, and I am truly engaged in expressing myself. This act of expressing myself is my reality.

The possibility exists that something will trigger one of these destructive core conditioned identifications. If I do not maintain awareness that this can happen, and thus be capable of acknowledging the reaction as it arises, I will be reacting to the conditioned identification. At these times, my awareness of myself in the moment sinks back into my conditioning, and I am reacting unconsciously and unable to write.

More often than not, surprisingly, at the completion of the writing session I feel satisfied and fulfilled. I love shutting down the computer. I will make a few calls, run a few errands, do a little reading, and then I often go to yoga to end the day. On the days that I do not feel satisfied with my writing session, I enter the cycling with the familiar self-disparaging thoughts and negative feelings, which may last nearly to the end of yoga class. Inevitably the process of practicing yoga breaks whatever destructive cycle I may have been engaged in when I entered the class. My mind is clear. My body is spent and relaxed, and I feel at peace. I drive home anticipating a lovely evening with my husband.

The evening is relaxing and nourishing. We have a nice long dinner together, talking and sharing. We listen to music, and then we watch a movie. I read a little before going to sleep, and then my husband rubs my back as I drift off to sleep.

SNAP OUT OF IT NOW! MOMENT

24 Hours

As a way to launch the inventory that you will be doing in the next chapter, take a 24-hour period in your life and begin to catalogue your everyday thoughts, judgments, actions and reactions. This exercise will help you bring to awareness the conditioned identifications that you live with, day in and day out. Don't get lost or become obsessive; just allow yourself to observe and write. I suggest setting aside 20 to 30 minutes for this exercise.

I have also found this to be a helpful exercise as a refresher when you are feeling stuck.

1. Pull out your journal, and find a quiet and comfortable space for the next 20 to 30 minutes.

2. Congratulate yourself for taking the time, energy, and courage to confront your conditioned identity.

3. Begin with a typical day. Start upon awakening in the morning and continue through each part of your day until you fall asleep in the evening. As your mind travels through the day, write down every thought, feeling, and action or reaction that occurs to you. Use my example above as a model.

This practice will be an ongoing gift to your increased awareness of your conditioned identifications. Remember, it is in the acknowledgment of the negative identifications that we become free of them.

Later you'll want to go back and think about your 24 hours. What are some of your reactions that you feel had a negative impact on your life? What are the elements that are causing you habitual distress?

- Did you spend a big part of your day ruminating on someone you feel has done you wrong?

- Did you yell at anyone?

- Did you feel stressed out?

- Did you feel overwhelmed?

- Did you feel depressed?

- Were you worried or anxious?

- Did you feel afraid?

When you are trying to identify the negative reactions that you want to change in your life, you might have impulses that will try to stop you. The four stages that keep you from being your own conditioner are:

As a way to target your professional relationships and to become more aware of how your conditioning influences the way you experience these relationships, it would be valuable to observe, witness, and document your thoughts, feelings, reactions and actions during a day at work. Try it out: take your journal to work with you one day and confront your conditioning with honesty and courage. Using the 24-hour model can also be very effective in your personal relationships. You may want to bring to your awareness how your conditioning is influencing the conflict you experience with your partner. As you get the hang of this, you'll find all sorts of opportunities for increasing self-awareness.

1. Denial that your life is determined by the conditioning. People deny that they are like their parents—deny that they are unconsciously conditioned to become, in many ways, like their parents. *I am not conditioned. I've consciously made my own choices!* This is even truer when the conditioned behavior is not clearly seen as stemming from the parent—the behavior itself may look very different from the parent's behavior.

2. Anger toward your conditioners. As people begin to see and acknowledge the way they are living their lives, they experience anger toward the people who they begin to see conditioned them in this way. If they do not deal with this anger, they remain justified in their anger and continue to unconsciously cycle with angry reactions—leading to the next stage.

3. Need to blame your conditioners: mother, father, older siblings or significant others. If you do not understand the nature of conditioning—that it takes place, mostly unconsciously, throughout the generations of your family (grandmother conditioned mother and mother conditioned me)—you will go on cycling with the need to blame others, and never get beyond your conditioning. People often engage thoughts such as, *What might have been if...?* In this way, they condition themselves to blame others for everything that goes wrong in their lives—and, thus never move beyond the blame game.

4. Need to ask *why, how, what, when, where?* People are conditioned to want to know the answers, and therefore we want to know why, when, and how they were conditioned to react negatively. They think that getting to the *why* will lead to feeling better, ending the cyclic questioning, and being capable of creating their desired life. Then, they do not understand why they are still living and reliving the same negative situations over and over again. In

the moment, asking why keeps you in an endless cycle: living life according to your conditioning and your traditional script.

Stop looking for another book, another therapist, or another gym! Start turning your focus inward for self-realization and move beyond your cyclic behaviors and actions. Stop worrying about everyone else. Start to focus on you!

When you are experiencing one of those inhibitors, you will want to take a Snap Out of It Now! moment and breathe with awareness of yourself in the present moment. When you turn your attention on other people, through denial, anger, blame or cycling, you lose focus within yourself. Here is an exercise to help you return to an inner focus and presence when you feel urged to respond to a negative conditioned identification or when you become aware that your are experiencing one of the four stages of self-avoidance:

SNAP OUT OF IT NOW! MOMENT

Moving Beyond Denial, Anger, Blame: Negative Cycling

Making the commitment to be self-aware and to break free from the walls of negative conditioning requires that you learn to notice and de-condition reactions of denial, anger, blame, and the desire to mentally understand rather than to viscerally experience.

Notice and observe yourself as you engage a negative reaction:

- Denial of responsibility: *It's not my fault.*

- Anger or resentment toward another person or the situation.

- Blaming someone else for the way you feel.

- Questioning: *Why does this always happen to me? Why do I feel hurt/angry/frustrated? Why do I always doubt myself?*

Acknowledge that these outward reactions are keeping you disconnected from the ability to recognize a negative identification, and disconnected from your inner experience—the key to ending the negative cycle—and thus disconnected from the experience of yourself in this moment.

Now, de-condition the outward reaction:

1. Acknowledge that your reaction—denial, anger, blame, questioning—is conditioned and therefore occurs automatically without your conscious awareness.

2. Experience yourself while you react. Stop, look, listen, and breathe. What is your personal awareness of yourself in this situation? Notice how your body is feeling.

3. Sense the feeling within your body. The outward reaction is provoked by an inner feeling. As you breathe, see if you can use your senses to locate and identify the feeling within your body. Allow your attention to remain with this sensation and experience the feeling fully for the first time.

4. Breathe to the sensation of the feeling—provoking denial, anger, blame, questioning—wherever it is in your body. As you breathe, feel your breath going to this area of your body. Your breath will release the

sensation, and as the sensation dissipates you are freed from the impulse to automatically react with denial, anger, blame, or questioning. You are present and aware in this moment.

ACCEPTANCE OF YOURSELF WITHIN THE CONDITIONING

The first step to becoming aware and accepting yourself within the conditioning is the acknowledgment that your current awareness is conditioned. It skews your point of view toward the negative and creates mental roadblocks to your happiness. You have accepted that you have been conditioned and that some of your conditioned reactions are negative, and you will be working on responding to negative reactions without denial, anger, blame and negative cycling. Each time you face a part of yourself that has negative elements, you are opening yourself to new possibilities for inner joy and you are taking another step closer to living the life of your dreams. As you actively participate with your conditioning, you are becoming your own conditioner.

You will need to identify, and inventory when possible, those specific elements of your conditioning that are holding you back. Now that you have a rough idea of what elements are holding you back from the initial 24 hours exercise, and know how to move past denial, anger, blame and negative cycling when recognized, the next step is to make the inventory of your conditioned identifications. Once you see the cause of your problems clearly, you can confront and move past them. The next chapter is about how to take an inventory of your conditioning.

CHAPTER TEN

Inventory of Core Conditioned Identifications

E ach of us has a core group of thoughts, judgments, beliefs, expectations, and stories that control how we move through life. This *inventory* is about the discovery of who we have been conditioned to be—our conditioned identity—and through our acceptance of this, we experience ourselves capable of becoming who we want to be.

AWARENESS OF CONDITIONING, AWARENESS OF THE SELF

For those of you who have no time: the time is now! The time has come to begin to list the core conditioned identifications that have become your identity. This list will put in black and white what rules your life: core conditioned identifications and their reactions. This inventory is in the here and now.

The point is to Snap Out of It Now! No more vacillating.

During your inventory creation, you will become aware of how conditioned identifications have determined your life experience: your relationship to your environment, to others, and to yourself.

Many encouraging and positive conditioned identifications will be realized, together with discouraging and negative conditioned identifications. The focus of the inventory is to bring to awareness those core conditioned identifications which are negative. They obstruct your ability to move forward in life and to live to your fullest potential.

Negative, core conditioned identifications are formed early in your personal development, often in childhood or young adulthood. With awareness of these inhibiting core conditioned identifications you will have the opportunity to become the agent of your own life, free to pursue your life goals unhindered. Many clients will initially resist doing this inventory, as they feel that bringing their negative thinking to awareness will empower the content of this thinking. Only when they proceed with their inventory do they realize that the opposite is true. When you become aware of your negative identifications, you take the power back and are in the position of creating new more creative, self-affirming, and life-enhancing thoughts.

All people make lists and inventories. Some lists are silently thought, while others are written down on paper. Some lists you create inventory your property or catalogue the groceries you need, but you also make more personal inventories: of needs and desires, of friends and those who support you, of productive and nonproductive behaviors, and of what disparages or encourages you. Whether or not you consciously realize it, these inventories help to determine your sense of self. Often people believe that making and modifying these lists can change who they are. These inventories are a healthy start. This chapter will help guide you in making an inventory of your life that helps you identify and confront your conditioning.

Before beginning your inventory, you must identify that you live within a conditioned process—everything you think, feel, sense, and do is conditioned.

You must accept the following:

1. I am conditioned.

2. I have formed conditioned identifications: thoughts, judgments, and beliefs.

3. My conditioned identifications have created a conditioned identity.

4. I am conditioned to react according to these conditioned identifications.

5. I cycle unconsciously with my reaction.

6. My awareness is conditioned such that while cycling I am living within the reality of my conditioned identification.

The most important inventory we must make is the inventory of our core conditioned identifications.

First of all, banish all thoughts you might have about the possible inadequacy of what you are about to put down on paper. Listen to and heed your positive thoughts. You are worth this time and energy. You are important. You are competent. You are good enough. Your voice has worth. Your problems are important. You are great, and your greatness can emerge.

When you start your inventory of conditioned identifications, you must first sort out which identifications cause the core problems, self-destructive thought processes and consequent self-destructive behaviors. There are millions of thoughts, judgments, perceptions, expectations, beliefs, and stories about yourself that occupy your mind, and while you might take the time to become aware of each and every one, it is the core, negative conditioned identifications that will be the focus in this inventory. They will be clear and persistent.

The process of confrontation may cause feelings of anxiousness and of being overwhelmed, but avoiding the anxiety is far worse than the confrontation. When repressed, negative emotions and identifications may manifest themselves as a physical malady, panic, or depression. You think—because you are conditioned to think—that when you avoid a negative emotion by projecting and blaming someone else, that you will feel better. The reality is that when feelings are not acknowledged and experienced, they will find a home within your body. The feeling will find a way to be expressed within the body: through headaches, tension in the neck or shoulders, or irritation in stomach and bowels.

SNAP OUT OF IT NOW! MOMENT

Relaxation

When you are doing your inventory and you find yourself feeling anxious, irritated, or angry, then take a break.

1. Acknowledge the negative emotion or identification.

2. *Stop, look,* and *listen* to the feeling sensation: tightness or heat in your chest or tummy; tension in your neck and shoulders, or any other discomfort in your body.

3. Breathe to the feeling sensation in your body.

4. When you feel ready, return to the inventory.

You may not immediately become aware of some of your conditioned identifications, as some are unconscious. However, you can focus your attention on the conditioned reactions in which you engage—irritation, blame, fear, jealousy—and thereby deduce your core conditioned identifications. Simply by identifying your emotional reactions, you can trace your source conditioning. In this way, you can begin the inventory of your core conditioned identifications.

I had a client, Jane, who was having difficulty uncovering her core conditioned identifications. Jane said that she had a strained relationship with her mother, but did not know why and felt uncomfortable with blaming her mother. I suggested that she pay close attention to how she reacted to her mother during their next visit with each other. Jane recognized that she always felt a slight irritation around her mother, and when she brought awareness to this reaction it became more intense: she felt anger. With a little exploration, she discovered that her mother frequently corrects her pronunciation of words or use of grammar, and this always makes Jane feel irritated. Now, Jane realizes that her reaction of irritation is directed toward herself and is provoked by her conditioned identification: *You are worthless, you can't even speak correctly.*

There is no need to worry about missing any core conditioned identifications. As you become more aware of yourself and your emotions, it becomes easier to identify the thoughts and judgments that have caused emotional reactions. And, remember to congratulate yourself often. You are doing the necessary work that will lead you out of negativity and into the life you have always dreamed about! While it is true that you have unconscious identifications, they will be uncovered. It simply is part of the process of self-awareness. It is a myth that there is something buried deeply in your unconscious and that without uncovering that one—the root of all your conditioning—then all is lost.

Breathe. You cannot miss. The root of all your conditioning is the simple fact that you are conditioned.

The process of making the inventory is self-generative. As the core conditioned identifications are listed, you will naturally become aware of others. Finally, unconsciously embedded core conditioned identifications will come to the forefront. This process is about bringing your core conditioned identifications to awareness so that you may live a life that is unconfined by your conditioning.

The core conditioned identifications are the key to exposing the conditioning in your thinking, feeling, doing, and choosing. You may experience difficulty in your efforts to look at yourself, as it is challenging and often painful to look at oneself and see the truth. After all, you are conditioned to pay attention to what society, culture and other individuals think—not to look for truth within yourself. As you begin your inventory, you may find that your most difficult thoughts, feelings, and sensations will begin to emerge, and the strength of these emotions may very well overwhelm you with their negativity. These are your most disturbing and inhibiting core conditioned identifications— created early in your youth, they hold more power—which block your efforts to create the life you want for yourself.

When you first begin, you may feel fear: fear that you will fail yourself or fail others, fear that your list will not work or that you have created it incorrectly. Breathe with the sensation of fear within your body. It is in your acknowledgment of fear that the fear will begin to point you to what is most important for you. Hang onto your inner strength. If you simply write down your feelings and experiences, you cannot go wrong. Nobody knows you better than you know yourself. If you get stuck, use the feelings to identify the thoughts or judgments provoking your feelings. Most importantly, don't give up. Your courage will reward you in the end. Confrontation will change your life for the better and help you become a stronger, happier, more balanced person living the life you have yet to only dream about.

Aided creative visualization, religious retreats, hypnosis and other spiritually enhancing tools can be helpful, but if you are using self-help vehicles to escape yourself, then you are wasting your time and money. Spiritual endeavors when used as escapes achieve only a temporary displacement of your sensibility into another person's or organization's haven of peace and contentment. To find your own lasting personal peace and contentment, turn within yourself and accept who you are and how conditioning has affected you. *Start by saying, I am conditioned. I am conditioned to react. I must identify and acknowledge my conditioned identifications and my reactions before I can begin a process that will change the experience of my day.*

WHEN I DO MY INVENTORY, I SEE MYSELF!

The inventory is the awareness of yourself within the conditioning. When you look at your inventory, you come face to face with your conditioned identifications and your conditioned reactions. In this moment of conscious confrontation you become liberated through awareness from the prison of conditioning, and free to become your own conditioner.

JUDGMENTS

In your inventory you will list your judgments. It is important to realize that the repeated judgments we make about ourselves and about others are conditioned, and have become our core conditioned identifications. We may think we share the same judgments as others, yet when we acknowledge our judgments we see that though they may be similar to those others have, they are indeed ours and have become our conditioned identifications. The judgments we hold toward ourselves are the hardest to confront, as they, being conditioned, are with us all the time. These judgments can pertain to anything about ourselves: *I am stupid; No one cares about me; I should be more creative, intelligent, or patient*—or on the more positive side, *I can do anything to which I set my mind; I am hardworking; I am honest.*

Our judgments, whether positive or negative, limit our ability to see the bigger picture. We are unable to see that which lies outside the confines of our own conditioned thinking. If we acknowledge our judgments as conditioned, we can expand our thinking to include more information. Making this inventory is not a way to make us better people, but rather a way to make us more aware of our conditioning and its impact upon our life, and thereby to open ourselves up to the possibility of changing our reactions to our core conditioned identifications—which can help us to feel better about ourselves.

In 2003, South Georgia businessman Dan Ponder received the JFK Profile in Courage award that grew out of a speech he made to Georgia lawmakers. As an elected state legislator of Georgia and a self-proclaimed descendant of slave owners, Dan spoke to his colleagues supporting the need for his state to send a message to people performing hate crimes toward minorities, gays, and others, "that Georgia has no room for hatred within its borders," and to pass a controversial hate-crimes bill.

In his speech to his state legislature, Mr. Ponder referred to a very important woman in his life who was black and whom he loved as his second mother. He stated that when he was 12 or 13, he stopped kissing her good-bye as he left for school. When she told him that the reason he no longer kissed her good-bye was because she was black, he rejected this, made excuses, but now told his colleagues how in that instant he knew she was right. He said that he denied that this was true, "But I was forced at that age to confront a small dark part of myself. I don't even know where it came from."

We see here how unaware we are of our own conditioning and the process by which we are conditioned. We also see in Dan Ponder's speech how acknowledgment of a conditioned identification—a racism against black people in Mr. Ponder's case—leads to the ability to choose our actions rather than continue to be controlled by our unconscious and predictable reactions (predictable because they are conditioned reactions). From Dan Ponder's acknowledgment of his own conditioning (to turn away from his black nanny), he was able to make a pledge to himself not to be prejudiced, saying "that never, ever again would I look in the mirror and know that I had kept silent, and let hate or prejudice or indifference negatively impact a person's life." We must list our core conditioned identifications, especially those that are ugly and humiliating for us to acknowledge, in order to stop being controlled by the behavioral, emotional and physical reactions they cause.

Take a few minutes to start listing your life judgments, either here or in your journal.

Judgments:

_____

_____

_____

_____

_____

_____

_____

PERCEPTIONS

Our perceptions are conditioned. Perceptions stem from what we sense—a gut feeling—and then we give meaning to this sensation. When we are introduced to a man who shakes our hand and then looks away, we immediately form a perception. We might think this person's eyes looking away signifies his rejection of us. We are conditioned to personalize our perceptions of others' reactions.

We find our core conditioned identifications by identifying the ways in which we perceive ourselves, our environment, and others. By looking closely at the perceptions we have of others, and conversely, of how others perceive us, we will become aware of how we have been conditioned to perceive ourselves (conditioned identifications). We may sense, when we are interacting with a friend, that this friend is not in synch with our manner or perception, or that they are not being sensitive to our feelings. Perhaps we perceive our friend as bored, self-absorbed, or insensitive. Our own conditioned experiences have guided our impression of our friend. We could not know, for instance, that our friend could be experiencing a sudden physical pain and could be silently trying to assess what might be wrong with him or herself. We understand other people's behavior only in terms of how we perceive—sense and interpret—their behavior, which is limited to what we experience and know ourselves.

Even our perception of what is painful, uncomfortable, or pleasurable is conditioned. What I may perceive as painful—sitting crossed legged in a lotus position—is very different from what

153

my yoga teacher perceives as painful. She meditates for some time in a lotus position. We are both conditioned to perceive pain differently as the comfort level of our minds and bodies are conditioned differently. Our perceptions represent the reality in which we live, and our reality is driven by our conditioned identifications. Therefore, we want to list our perceptions in the inventory.

Perceptions:

_____
_____
_____
_____
_____
_____
_____
_____

EXPECTATIONS

Our expectations are conditioned, and this is another category of core conditioned identifications that will be included in our inventory. We have expectations of ourselves, of others, and even of God—or of a spiritual nature. We expect ourselves to act a certain way, and we expect people to act a certain way toward us. We may expect, for example, that if we work hard we will prosper; that there is a level playing field; and that our parents or our partner will always be there for us. We may have stopped or wanted to stop expecting anything, if we believe our expectations have failed us. After all, we all have wishes, hopes, desires, and entitlements, but they sometimes go unnoticed and do not always come true. We may not think of these as expectations. We wish for a new job opportunity; we hope that we will get pregnant; we desire harmonious relationships; and we feel entitled to be happy. Often, we are not aware that our wishes, hopes, dreams, and desires have become expectations. These are hidden expectations, as when we wish or hope for something, we are not conscious that we are truly expecting to have our wish come true. When unacknowledged, they continue to reinforce our conditioned awareness and therefore we have no control over how these core conditioned identifications affect our life.

For example, a client of mine named Pam uncovered one of her hidden expectations, *No matter what I do things will turn out badly.* In the process of creating her inventory, she realized the inhibiting force this expectation had on her life and was able to see that she had been conditioned to expect the worst for herself. With her acknowledgment, Pam began to see how she had been reinforcing this expectation through her unawareness of it. With her newfound awareness, Pam was able to realize all the things that were going right for her, and that she could control and utilize her awareness to her advantage!

Try to think of at least one of your expectations in life. You can continue this exercise in your journal.

Expectations:

_____

_____

_____

_____

_____

_____

_____

STORIES

Our core conditioned identifications will also be found in the stories we tell others and the stories we tell ourselves. When we write out our stories, we will see our core conditioned identifications arise from the story. If we listen carefully, these stories rarely change. Maybe we add more interesting ideas, but the theme remains the same. As we continue telling the story, the conditioning is reinforced. We may not even be aware that we are telling our story as we talk to people. We may be aware of our repetition in the stories we tell, but we do not acknowledge this repetitive theme as our conditioning. When we become aware of the theme of our stories, we are exposing the core conditioned identifications.

By writing down and cataloguing the themes of our stories, we can determine how we have become who we are, what we have accomplished, and what we want to accomplish. Our core conditioned identifications create the stories of our lives. We may attempt to stop telling the stories of our lives. Or, we may seek out the help of someone—a therapist, mentor, parent, or older sibling—who we believe knows our story or who can help us find the facts so we can rewrite it. Despite the difficulty of acknowledging the core conditioned identifications that have in essence created our story, we cannot rewrite our stories. We must force ourselves, with help when necessary, to list the core conditioned identifications that have created our story. Through this inventory, we can become aware of our stories and actively decide how we will continue participating in them. We cannot rewrite the past, but we can create new stories for our future as we become our own conditioners.

What is one of your stories?

Stories we live by:

_____

_____

_____

_____

_____

_____

_____

CULTURAL CONDITIONING: BELIEFS, IDEAS, ETHICS AND VALUES

Each of us has perceptions about how our culture has affected us. Our family heritage, and the stories we hear about our ancestors, will also condition us. The socio-economic or geographic environment in which we live—Los Angeles versus San Francisco—will condition us too. The state, region, and country in which we live will all have their conditioning effects upon us. Whether we were brought up in a beach community versus a desert community will also have uniquely conditioning effects.

The regional food we eat, and the music we listen to, are conditioners. Each culture has its own rituals surrounding all the practices of living. Each of us as individuals believes our culture has affected us, and thus we have formed conditioned identifications relating to the effects of our culture, whether or not we are aware of them.

I have always loved the ocean and the beach culture. When I was a child and my family came to La Jolla for the summer I remember telling myself, *I will always live by the beach. I will raise my children so that they will be able to play in the ocean every day.* I remember thinking that I could not redo my childhood, but I could create the childhood I wanted for my children. Even though I've never had children, and currently live in the mountains, I still have the core belief that when I am at the ocean I am more connected with myself and more alive. I love the little towns along the coast where there are surf shops, little restaurants, and people walking in shorts, bathing suits, and flip flops. I love going to get a burrito or sandwich after hours of surfing, and the feeling of being a part of this wonderful culture that is so free and easy. I love just driving up the coast listening to music, checking out the waves, and watching people swimming and playing in the water. I love the way the sunshine and the moisture in the air feel on my skin. I love diving into a wave just as it begins to break, and the way my body feels as it is tossed and turned by the currents in the water.

When I am in the mountains, particularly when there is no snow, I react with a feeling of being boxed in. This reaction is provoked by my core identification that, *I am connected, alive, and happier when living near the ocean.* You may think it natural for me to love the ocean. You might say, "Adrianne just prefers living by the ocean, just as I prefer living in the city." What we do not realize is that we have been conditioned to prefer the ocean or the city, and our feeling of discomfort, or tension, while in another environment is our reaction to our conditioning.

We have culturally conditioned, core conditioned identifications that are self-supportive, such as a healthy and productive work ethic, a spiritual belief system, and a code of ethics. There are also culturally conditioned identifications that are not self-supportive and that actually lead to feelings of exhaustion, self-dissatisfaction, and self-worthlessness, such as the self-judgments of incompetence in one or more areas of one's life—*I am not smart/thin/rich enough*—or the belief that more is better, which has resulted in our culture's overuse and abuse of foods, drugs, alcohol, work, and exercise.

Cultural conditioning—beliefs, ideas, ethics and values:

_____

_____

_____

_____

_____

_____

_____

CORE CONDITIONERS: WE BECOME OUR PARENTS

In making our inventory we will experience certain thoughts, behaviors, feelings, and sensations that remind us of our core conditioners. When Alex was visiting his mother, or even talking with her on the phone, he was struck with the similarity between the way she thought and felt about the day, life, and other people and the way Alex himself had become aware that he thought about his day, his life's progress, and his manner of perceiving others. If we look closely at ourselves we will see the same core conditioned identifications, and conditioned reactions as part of our interactions with ourselves and with others, as we have observed in our core conditioner.

When Alex felt lonely, rather than picking up the phone and calling a friend, he would remain alone and wonder why a friend was not calling him. What he realized was that this was the same way his mother reacted to feelings of loneliness; his mother's core conditioned identification had become his. He would think to himself, *When I feel lonely others should reach out to me*, provoking reactions of anger toward others for not reaching out to him. We protest too much by saying, *I am not like my mother/father,* and *I have changed my thoughts, beliefs, habits, judgments, and expectations.* In fact, the saying is often true, and we often share the same core conditioned identifications that we see in our core conditioners. Rather than fighting the facts, recognize them so that you can change and not fall into the same emotional traps that have plagued your ancestors.

Like Alex, my mother is my main, core conditioner. I am aware of how I have identified with many of the likes and dislikes that I perceived were held and are held by my mother. I disliked the town I grew up in because I perceived my mother disliked it. It wasn't until late in high school that I finally began to appreciate the things that this small town had to offer. I was so focused on how boring and unsophisticated the town was that I didn't have any room within my consciousness to appreciate the beauty of the desert landscape at sunset, or the kind and friendly openness of the people in the community.

Those core conditioned identifications closed me off from enjoying, or even seeing, the potential beauty or pleasures that the little desert community might have offered. I was aware of my perception of my mother's dislike of that small town and I was aware that I developed a similar dislike. I was not aware that I was being conditioned and that I was developing a core conditioned identification with the dislike of all small and desert towns. As long as I would not acknowledge this as a core conditioned identification, I unconsciously slipped into my conditioning, which is what one might call being natural. When asked where I lived when traveling, I responded from my conditioning and defensively said, "I live in the Reno/Tahoe area. I live there for the skiing." Then, later, I would feel embarrassed at my defensiveness and realize that I was trapped in the core conditioned identification that was determined by my earlier conditioning.

In making your inventory, you will list your core conditioners—mother, father, siblings, grandparents, teachers, peers—so you can be aware of the core conditioner's conditioned identifications, and see that you have many of the same. We may find it difficult to come up with the conditioned identifications we perceive in our core conditioners, but it is often easy to identify their conditioned reactions. What we are really after here is the discovery of our own core conditioned identifications. Using the reactions we observe in our core conditioners will help us become aware of our own conditioned reactions, and therefore lead us to our core conditioned identifications.

People often blame their core conditioners—usually their parents—for their conditioned identifications and conditioned reactions, especially when it becomes apparent that these identifications and reactions have been passed on to them. What people often fail to realize is that our core conditioners were likewise conditioned, unaware of the conditioning that their parents passed on to them, and unaware that they perpetuated our social conditioning. It is natural for us to want to blame our conditioners, but we must come to understand that unlike linear problems like termites, that can be solved by destroying the cause or root of the problem, people and their families or other support network are connected in a multitude of ways, have web-like problems, and need nurturing and understanding to grow from their traumas. Destruction of a relationship or denigration of another person who you feel has caused you harm will only make life worse for everyone, including you. Once upon a time our parents or other salient figures helped form our sense of reality, including both the positive and the negative, but today is not the day to start pointing fingers, it is the day to recognize the parts of our conditioned identity that we have found hard to face, and take charge of the future of our identity and reality. We should not despair just because we can neither destroy nor change the people who helped form us early in life. By identifying the behaviors they passed onto us, we can find a new way of life for ourselves.

We Are Our Children's Mirrors

We want to condition our children so that they do well in school, establish healthy friendships, participate in the family with responsibility and love, and have the greatest opportunity to create happy and successful lives for themselves. What we don't realize is that unless we confront our own conditioning, we will unconsciously condition our children with our own unconscious conditioned identifications, just as we have been conditioned with our parents' conditioned identifications. We consciously intend to condition our children to have a positive outlook, to behave with honesty and responsibility, to do their homework, and to care about others. And yet, if we are not aware of our own core conditioned identifications that provoke reactions of depressiveness, dishonesty, irresponsibility, or self-absorption, then whether we like it or not—and whether we intend otherwise or not—our children will indeed be conditioned by our core conditioned identifications.

Unless we are aware of our own problems which can affect our children's actions, we will continue to be frustrated and disturbed when our child mirrors our own destructive or self-destructive behaviors. We wonder why the talks we have had with our child, or our disciplining efforts, or the therapy we have begun do not seem to have the effect we want on our child's behavior. The conditioning is so powerful that it will continue to control our own reactions to others and to situations, just as it will control the way our children begin to react to people and situations.

Christina shared with me her confusion and disturbance when her daughter was dishonest about her schoolwork and life in general. Christina had long talks with her daughter about dishonesty, and at the end of each of the talks she felt convinced that her daughter would change her behavior. Unfortunately, the lying and dishonesty continued. The problem was that Christina was not acknowledging her own conditioning with regard to honesty and responsibility. She would often talk on the phone while driving her daughter to school and say things that her daughter was aware were untrue, and she would habitually lie to her ex-husband—her daughter's father. Christina was sending her daughter mixed signals. Verbally, she was telling her daughter to be honest. But in action, she was communicating that dishonesty was acceptable when the result would be positive for you, or if you disliked the person with whom you were communicating. Christina was unaware that her thoughts, feelings, expectations, actions, and reactions were impacting and conditioning the way her daughter behaved and reacted, regardless of the number of disciplinary speeches or actions telling her daughter to act differently than her mother.

As in Christina's case, so it may also be in our observance of our child's behaviors (conditioned reactions) that we become aware of our own core conditioned identifications and conditioned reactions. It is often said, "The apple doesn't fall far from the tree." It is also true that the tree is never far from the apple.

What similarities do you see between your parents or other core conditioners and yourself?

Conditioned identifications of core conditioners:

_____

_____

_____

_____

_____

_____

_____

FANTASY

What is it that you fantasize about? Where does the content of your fantasy life originate? Are you seeking the perfect partner? Do you want to make a million dollars? Do you seek sexual experimentation? Do you secretly want to be famous? Whatever your fantasies entail, they arise out of your conditioning, and are often engaged in your efforts to avoid, or attempt to overcome, the conditioning within which you live your life.

From as early as I can remember I was attracted to and intrigued by beautifully decorated and designed homes. I remember my mother telling me stories when I was a young child of the very beautiful and large homes or estates she visited in Europe when she was a young woman. As a child, I would fantasize that when I grew up I would have a home that was similar to ones I admired in the films that I saw. One can see quite easily the core conditioned identification of my fantasy: *I shall live in a uniquely beautiful home.* Even though my current home is comfortable and very pleasing to me, if I was not aware of this core conditioned identification, I would react with jealousy and envy when I am invited to a friend's uniquely beautiful home. I might find something about my friend's home that I could criticize. Awareness of this core conditioned identification allowed me to acknowledge these potential reactions and therefore not close myself off from admiring and enjoying a beautiful home that is not my own.

While making our inventory, you will use your fantasies to help uncover your core conditioned identifications. Until then, you will not know that even your fantasies are conditioned, and you will not know that your fantasies will reveal your core conditioned identifications.

What do you fantasize about?

Fantasy:

_____

_____

_____

_____

_____

_____

_____

As you continue with your inventory, more conditioned identifications will come to your awareness and you will hear the core conditioned identifications—those that repeat over and over again—that dominate and control your life. The inventory will soon be experienced as organic; as you add to it you become aware of what you have been leaving out. Eventually, you will discover the theme of your conditioning. A theme of your story will emerge from the conditioned identifications in your inventory. The theme will have been consistent throughout your life, and now you have the opportunity to make some adjustments to it as you uncover your unconditioned true self-experience, the joy of consciously creating the theme of your life!

The theme of my conditioning was, *Words get in the way of my desire to express.* Having fully acknowledged my conditioned identifications, I no longer deny or reject my desire to discover, clarify, express, and be acknowledged for the expression of my voice. The inhibitors that constituted my reality in the past are now checked by my personal agency, my choice to embrace my wants and needs. I no longer rationalize why I don't have the time to write. Instead, I sit down to write each day. My voice is an expression of my inner power, and connected with my inner power, I am strong both inside and out. By acknowledging that which inhibited me in the past, I have been set free. I tell you not only as a doctor, but as a friend: you can do it too!

Your inventory will help you acknowledge the core conditioned identifications that are getting in your way, and allow you to actively remove the roadblocks to your success. Using your inventory will allow you to recognize and stop the defeating cycling caused by negative conditioning. You will become capable of choice where you once felt no choices were available to you, and you will become more open to the experiences available to you in the living present. With the acknowledgment that your identity is conditioned comes the awareness that you have the potential to become your own conditioner from this moment on. Don't wait to have your life handed back to you, take back your life now!

SNAP OUT OF IT NOW! MOMENT

Charting Your Conditioning

1. Get your trusty journal, and divide a page or pages into two sections.

2. On one side, make a list of the negative attributes about yourself you would like to change and the negative attributes you see in other people that you would like to see changed, as well as the judgments, perceptions, expectations, stories, cultural conditioners, and fantasies, that you feel may be affecting you negatively. If you feel stuck, refer back to this chapter as a reference, or to the previous writing exercises you have done for ideas.

3. On the other side, make a corresponding list of how you would like to feel without the effects of these conditioned hindrances, and how you see yourself without these elements of your conditioning that are disturbing, self-limiting, or destructive. You can continue to revise and add to this list, but it is important to find your starting point and begin the process of becoming aware of the conditioning specific to you. Identifying what is holding you back will enable you to break free of your conditioning and see yourself for who you are and who you want to be, as opposed to who other people want you to be or have conditioned you to be.

4. After working on your list, take some time to meditate on the work you have done. *Stop*, *look*, and *listen* to the process of confrontation, acknowledgment, and acceptance! *Breathe*—become aware of your breath as you confront, acknowledge and accept your conditioning. Awareness does not come easily, but you have the inner power to become aware and take control of your life. Recognize and feel good about the fact that you have done so.

CHAPTER ELEVEN

The Snap Out of It Now! Method

This is the practice of awakening to the conditioning, identifying your conditioned thinking and reacting, choosing your actions, and becoming your own conditioner—four steps to inner joy!

Acknowledge your conditioning.

Inventory your conditioned identifications.

De-condition your conditioned reactions.

Become your own conditioner—connect with your inner joy and authentic self.

Now that you have completed your inventory of conditioned identifications, do you feel more connected with yourself? Perhaps you feel as Joseph Campbell expressed it: the rapture of being alive. You have taken steps that the majority of people in our world still choose to not to take on the path of self-awareness. You have crossed the threshold into awareness, and are on your journey to fully embracing your inner truth and experiencing inner joy!

By directly and honestly confronting the conditioning that has created who you are, you have faced your conditioned identity!

Joseph Campbell:

People say that what we're all seeking is a meaning for life. I don't think that's what we're really seeking. I think what we're seeking is an experience of being alive, so that our life experiences on the purely physical plane will have resonances within our own innermost being and reality, so that we actually feel the rapture of being alive.

But don't stop now. You are going to need to continue working with this new self-awareness. The conditioning has been reinforced throughout your entire life, so in order to break free from it and become your own conditioner you will need to practice the Snap Out of It Now! method and make it a part of your life. As you incorporate the Snap Out of It Now! method into your life, you are de-conditioning your negative reactions, you are becoming your own conditioner—a powerful, active and ongoing role.

Here are two powerful things to remember as you transition into living the life of your dreams. First of all, remember that the Snap Out of It Now! method is not about taking control as much as it is about releasing yourself from the control that your conditioning—those naysaying voices from your past—has had upon your experience. You don't need to force yourself to be what anyone else wants you to be; you do need to embrace your new understanding of yourself and go with it. Secondly, remember that the Snap Out of It Now! method is not about becoming someone else. The Snap Out of It Now! method is about becoming truly you through the awareness of your thoughts, your feelings, and your reactions; the awareness of your whole self that enables you to detoxify yourself of the negative thinking and behaviors that hinder you. In going through the exercises in this book, you have already come a long way, and as you follow the Snap Out of It Now! method, life is just going to keep getting better.

THE ONGOING PROCESS OF AWARENESS AND CHOICE

You are not naturally predisposed to knowing that it is your conditioned reactions that are keeping you from reaching your full potential, nor are you predisposed to de-conditioning these reactions. The Snap Out of It Now! method is a way of living with awareness of yourself in the present moment, choosing your actions consciously, de-conditioning reactions that no longer serve you, and remaining connected to yourself, others, and God/the Universe/the Mystery. Practicing this method, each day you will feel a little bit better, a little bit stronger, and a little more centered—and a lot closer to the experience of your inner joy! Remember that when you approach the act of de-conditioning a reaction, you need to make a commitment to *stop*, *look*, and *listen* to how you have been conditioned to react. Your gut reaction may be that you don't like the way you notice yourself reacting. It takes an honest, courageous effort to allow yourself to see what you might not want to see, because reactions that stem from anger and blame can be ugly. But just think of how much better you will feel—free to live your dreams—when you are purged of these negative reactions!

When you deny or avoid your reactions as you are conditioned to do, you will continue to cycle through them until finally you begin using the Snap Out of It Now! method to confront your reactions and experience the feeling that lies beneath them. Continuing to immerse yourself in a cycle of negative emotions and reactions is as unhealthy for you—as it is for everyone else around you—and eventually you will not be able to tolerate the venom of negative emotions coursing through your veins. When you recognize a negative reaction, it's okay to say, *This is me. I am reacting according to my conditioning, and I can change my reaction.* Making the shift from a negative to a positive reaction will be a relief, and will remove the stress inherently manifested by the negative emotion that has been suppressed through engagement with the reaction. Everything from your charisma to your immune system will improve dramatically through the simple power of progressive thinking. These subtle changes in the way you experience yourself and the choice of actions to everyday occurrences will cause a butterfly effect of positive rewards in every area of your life. The subtlety of the changes becomes astonishing in your experience of them. So when you're not sure if you can face a negative reaction, take a deep breath, do a quick Snap Out of It Now! moment and realize that there isn't anything wrong with you; there is simply a healthier, better way for you to react to be the best person you can be. Celebrate the positive changes you are making!

In this book, you are learning to de-condition the reactions that you have been conditioned to engage. Let's review the steps to de-conditioning.

1. Acknowledging "I am conditioned to react."

The Practice of de-conditioning requires that you sit down and look at yourself in the mirror and acknowledge your conditioning. Until you wake up to your conditioning, the reactions you engage are the only way you can react. As you see yourself with this new awareness, you are experiencing a shift in your thinking. You now know who you are, and it is time to begin the work with this new understanding.

2. Experiencing yourself reacting.

To de-condition a reaction, you have to experience the reaction first. You acknowledge your behavioral reaction and how it impacts your experience of yourself.

3. Sensing the feeling within the body.

Observe and witness your inner experience: the feeling within your body. Acknowledge that this inner feeling is triggering the outward reaction. As long as you continue reacting, you are disconnected from the inner feeling and disconnected from yourself.

4. Breathing to the feeling sensation in your body.

As you breathe mindfully, you are connecting with yourself—the feeling within your body—in the present moment. No longer do you feel the impulse to engage the negative reaction. You experience the freedom to choose your actions. You have become your own conditioner.

The practice of de-conditioning allows you to become capable of moving consciously beyond the limitations imposed by your conditioning. It is the awareness of your breath that is the key to de-conditioning your reactions. When you are aware of your breath, you are present in this moment: you are aware. You are capable of acting and reacting in ways that are not determined by your conditioning. The power of control in your life has now been shifted back to you.

DE-CONDITIONING: BECOMING AWARE OF HOW YOUR BODY EXPRESSES YOUR FEELINGS

The practice of de-conditioning can be challenging at times. It is about experiencing your whole self, including feelings of fear, anger, jealousy, self-hatred, joy, happiness, appreciation and love, and being capable of choosing how you will respond to the circumstances and people in your life. When you de-condition a reaction, you acknowledge yourself and the feelings that arise within your body. As you experience the inner feeling you choose how—or if—you want to react to the feeling. By making your reaction a mindful, active process, you are no longer controlled by your conditioned reactions. In this way, you resolve the feeling or state of mind that provokes the reaction. Eventually being connected to yourself—your inner experience—and consciously choosing to react in ways that generate inner joy will become conditioned, or as they say, second nature.

Within the practice of de-conditioning, you are anchoring yourself within the acknowledgment that you are conditioned. You identify with the conditioning, and are conditioned to react accordingly. You begin to learn a unique kind of self-control. When you experience yourself engaging a reaction such as anger, blame, or impatience, you will say to yourself, *I do not want to be an angry, disparaging, or impatient person. I want to be able to stop myself when I begin to react in these ways.* A common mistake that people make in the de-conditioning process is that they think to themselves, *I don't want to react badly: I want to be more patient,* for example, and thus avoid the critical step of acknowledging the conditioned reaction. You now know better! You know that they who avoid facing their negative reactions move only further away from the ability to react differently. Instead, you will think to yourself, *What is the specific behavior that I seek to change?* As some of my last words of advice to you, I wish you to continue to look at yourself honestly and to bear witness to your behaviors without judging yourself negatively in order to initiate positive change. However, when you catch yourself judging yourself: *stop, look,* and *listen.* Acknowledge your conditioned reaction to judge yourself, and then, breathe to the feeling in your body that provokes the impulse to judge yourself. Seeing yourself—both the good and the bad—is brave and powerful, and everyone is capable of this powerful self-awareness.

A client shared with me that when she was alone and had time on her hands she didn't know what to do with herself. At first, she said, *I really need to learn how to relax when I am alone.* In fact, what she really needed was to acknowledge how she was reacting—her tension and rigidity—when she had a day off. With awareness of the specific negative reactions, she was then able to de-condition her reaction and in this way experience herself as more relaxed.

You will need to resist trying to use willpower to stop your negative reactions. We are such rational animals that we try to use our intellect to figure out why we react a certain way, thinking that once we understand our reactions we will no longer need to engage them; or we see the cause for our reactions and see our reactions as the logical effect and believe that all we need to do is understand or avoid the cause. Someone might even say, "I have been programmed by my father/mother/sibling to react with anger and blame toward others." Remember that understanding can be positive, but mere understanding does not change negative behaviors. If you allow yourself to become totally absorbed in the causal factors that led to your reaction, you will begin to feel justified, thinking you had no choice in how you reacted. The truth is that regardless of why you react the way you do, you are always responsible for your actions. Keep in mind that more important than analyzing and understanding the reasons why you react the way you do is changing the way you react in your life right now. You can choose to wake up to your conditioning, de-condition your reactions, experience conscious choice and become your own conditioner!

THE POWER OF RESPONSIBLE REACTION IN THE PRESENT AND IN THE FUTURE

You have learned that you are conditioned, and that your conditioning determines who you are. You want to participate in the way your life unfolds. To do so, you have begun to learn how to snap out of your resistant and negative conditioning using this book as your guide. This is probably the first time that you have faced the mental pathways of your conditioning. You are now aware of how you may have denied, avoided, or rationalized elements of your conditioning in an effort to protect yourself from being aware of your negative reactions and from having to take responsibility for yourself and for your life. The challenge you will face, now and in the future, is to continue to grow in self-awareness, and this means to take full responsibility for your conditioning, yourself, and your life! It is not enough to say, "I am responsible for my thoughts, feelings, and actions." In order to live your life with conscious awareness and thus create the life you want, you will need to practice acknowledging your conditioning and de-conditioning your resistant and negative conditioned reactions. It is repetition that created your current conditioned reality; it will be repetition of the Snap Out of It Now! method that will guide you to a quantum leap out of your conditioned mind-set and to living with purpose, joy, and excellence!

Taking responsibility for your reactions is not easy. People do not really want to acknowledge that they could be negative in any way. Nobody wants to be "the bad one". And if you already knew you had problems, you might have hoped someone else would fix you. When you start to face your conditioning, you realize that the real change comes from within. You realize that it is up to you to begin the work of de-conditioning in order to break out of your confining conditioned reality. It can be a painful process, but the rewards are infinite and far outweigh any temporary discomfort you may experience along the way. The end result justifies the means!

It may seem overwhelming when you think about de-conditioning a pattern of reactions that you can see has roots in your very earliest relationships. You may find yourself thinking that you will have to go all the way into your past and work your way forward, and that this will take forever. Too much work. Too much time. What is occurring now is what has always occurred. Don't let your conditioning get in your way and stop you! When you are aware of how you are reacting in the present moment, you are dealing with your conditioned reaction that was programmed into you as a child. You need not dig back into your past. Your conditioned reactions are repetitive and will always present themselves when you take time to stop, look, and listen with a more intense focus. Instead of dwelling on the past, bring your attention back to the present. In the following exercise, using your senses and the power of the breath, experience yourself returning to present moment awareness.

SNAP OUT OF IT NOW! MOMENT

Listening to the Breath

1. Settle into a comfortable position.

2. Close your eyes.

3. Acknowledge a shifting of attention from your thinking mind to your breath.

---

4. Focus your attention on the breath and become aware of your breathing.

5. Listen to your breathing.

6. Listen to your breath as it goes in and out through your nose and mouth.

7. Notice that in the moment you are listening, you are not thinking. You are aware, but you are not thinking.

8. Notice that as you listen to your breathing, your attention is completely in the present moment.

9. You are right here, right now!

10. Stay with your breath as long as you like.

11. When you are ready gently open your eyes.

De-conditioning is a process. Sometimes it works the very first time and, astonishingly, you are freed from your conditioned reaction. Other times, you may go through the steps again and again in response to a negative reaction you identify until one day it clicks, and the cord to your reaction is severed. The more negative reactions you confront and de-condition, the better you will feel, the more happiness and inner peace you will attain, the more truly yourself and innately wise you will become. The process is unending as are the benefits!

INTEGRATING THINKING, EXPERIENCING, SENSING, AND BREATHING TO STOP NEGATIVE CYCLING

The practice of de-conditioning is the secret tool of the Snap Out of It Now! method. Once you are free of your negative reaction, you are fully capable of snapping out of your negative and resistant conditioning. Take the de-conditioning process one step at a time. Acknowledge who you are, experience yourself reacting, sense the feeling within the body, and as you breathe to your inner feeling experience yourself connecting with your deeper self and being released from the control of your conditioned reaction.

THE PRACTICE OF DE-CONDITIONING

Step 1: Acknowledge Yourself

Each morning after waking up, sit down in front of the mirror, make these acknowledgments and make de-conditioning a part of your daily routine.

Let me tell you, when I first started to sit in front of the mirror and acknowledge my conditioning, initially I would get bored or distracted, and then the next day or two I would only think of the process fleetingly, while brushing my teeth or driving to work. Then, as I became more frustrated with my reactions, I would realize that I must sit down in front of my mirror and acknowledge my conditioning with a focus on the present moment. Anything less and I would create stress within myself, rather than balance.

Soon, I began to experience the effectiveness of my self-acknowledgments and by doing this every day, I was eventually able to recognize my reactions as they arose during the day, acknowledge the reactions, and de-condition them quickly and effectively. You don't have to loose part of your day anymore to unconscious negative cycling.

SNAP OUT OF IT NOW! MOMENT

Self-Acknowledgment Mirror

1. Sit down, look at yourself in the mirror, and acknowledge the following:

2. I have been conditioned.

---

3. My conditioned identifications are ingrained in my mind.

4. My conditioned identifications determine my reactions and, in this way, rule my life

5. My conditioned reactions lead me into negative cycles of anger, blame, fear, anxiety, or depression.

6. I have not been conditioned to de-condition my reactions and end the cycle of reaction.

7. If I live this day with self-awareness and focus within the present moment, I have the power to recognize and de-condition my negative reactions and experience inner joy.

Until you can get up in the morning every day and confront your conditioned identity, you will be trapped by your conditioned reactions. You will be depriving yourself of seeing the choices available to you, reaching your potential as a human being, and experiencing the depth of joy that exists within you. So start today! Your life's passions and dreams are ready for the taking.

Step 2: Experience Your Reactions

When you are reacting, you are not aware of your breathing. You do not naturally experience your reaction. You need to experience the reaction that you want to de-condition. Being aware of what is happening within your body while you are engaging a conditioned reaction—feelings of tightness, rigidity, pain, warmth, pleasure, and so on— allows you to connect with your experience, and thus to evaluate the experience: *Does this action feel congruent with my inner truth?* When you can consciously witness and observe yourself reacting, and no longer willfully trying to stop or change the way you're reacting, you are ready to stop the cycle and de-condition the reaction.

As discussed, it isn't necessary or desirable to try to understand why you are reacting the way you are in the present moment. Doing so will only form justifications and rationalizations. Instead, pay attention to the feeling within you, such as confusion or fear, and the outward expression that is linked with this feeling—the conditioned reaction such as anger or blame. You may not want to accept that you are reacting in a negative way, and that this negative reaction is the result of your conditioning—a part of who you are. Therefore, you may have urges to deny, avoid and rationalize your conditioned reactions. This is where your commitment to self-awareness comes in again; review the last Snap Out of It Now! moment in chapter 9.

Don't waste your time with the cause. Instead, realize that this is you in the present moment, reacting in a way that is causing negativity in your life. Accept without blaming yourself or others that your reaction is the only way you could have reacted with that mindset, because it was how you were conditioned to react. The past is over, and you cannot change it. Stay with the present and experience yourself while reacting. Now that you are aware of the feeling and the negative reaction, you can condition yourself to act otherwise—now and in the future.

SNAP OUT OF IT NOW! MOMENT

Becoming Aware of the Experience

1. The next time you are in conversation with another person, *stop, look,* and *listen* to what is happening within you.

2. Listen to your inner body, even while talking or listening to the other person.

3. Begin to notice the sensations that arise within you when talking with a friend, a coworker, your boss, your parent, your child and your lover.

4. Notice the sensations within your body the next time you enter into a disagreement or argument with another person.

5. As soon after this experience as possible, pull out your journal and write about your experience as descriptively as you can. Focus on feelings, emotions, physical sensations, and areas of your body. Do not worry about labeling the feeling; describe the feeling as imaginatively as you can. This will increase your awareness of self—physically and emotionally—enhancing awareness of your inner experience.

Step 3: Sense the Feeling within Your Body

When you unconsciously engage a conditioned reaction, you are not experiencing yourself in the moment. You are not aware of the reaction your body is having in response to the feeling. In the moment, the cyclic thinking process—understanding, analyzing, judging, questioning—turns your attention to other people and keeps you from sensing the feeling within your body. When you shift your attention inward by becoming aware of your breathing, and attempt to notice and then sense the feelings within, you will find the awareness you seek.

The way to stay with your feelings is through the remarkable healing power of breath. When you notice a sensation within your body, you can use the power of your breath to sense—listen, touch, smell, see, and taste—the inner feeling. Becoming familiar with the process of sensing leads you towards increasing self-awareness and helps you get in touch with what you want. Sensing is part of the total experience of de-conditioning.

During the course of treatment, my client Joan said to me, "I am angry. I want you to know that I am no longer going to deny what I am feeling, and I am feeling angry because of something that you did." With this statement, though it may seem that Joan was acknowledging her anger, she was actually acknowledging her perception that I was responsible for her anger. Joan was feeling anger and as she reacted with an accusation, her thinking, *Dr. A made me angry, and I am justified in being angry because she was wrong,* was inhibiting her from sensing the feeling of anger that arose in her body. Joan would repeatedly blame others for the feelings that arose within her, and by doing this she never allowed herself to experience her own feelings and move on with her life. She was fed up with getting into hard-to-resolve situations and never feeling acceptance or intimacy.

As we talked through her feelings, she realized the reproachful behavior was a negative reaction she would have over and over again when she felt angry. She was then able to acknowledge the negative reaction that she needed to de-condition. Since she realized she was unable to sense her feelings, we began a practice of body awareness through breathing exercises. The next time we got together, Joan shared an experience she had at work where she became aware of herself feeling angry: she felt, or sensed, heat rising in her chest. Just before she felt herself begin to react by complaining about a coworker, she stopped and sat down at her desk. At her desk, she started to become aware of her breath. As she began to sense the experience within her body she noticed that along with the heat in her chest she felt tension in her neck and a sensation of tightness within her muscles. Joan started to become distracted by her ruminating on the annoyance of her coworker, but instead she stopped, breathed, and identified the feeling in her body as anger, which she realized she no longer wished to harbor. She told me that she was surprised by her experience because she said she no longer felt the need to reprimand her coworker.

It may be that after you acknowledge your conditioning, the experience of the reaction, and sense the feeling of anger within your body, your negative feelings, such as anger, will dissipate as they did for Joan in this situation. In the moment of acceptance of the feeling, you may stop experiencing the desire to become defensive or blame someone else for his or her behavior. Even though Joan felt good about her de-conditioning experience, she did realize that she needed to continue practicing de-conditioning, as she had been conditioned to react with blame in many situations.

SNAP OUT OF IT NOW! MOMENT

Shift Away from Another

1. *Stop, look,* and *listen*—stop ruminating on the other person or people.

2. Take a deep breath.

3. Acknowledge your conditioning.

4. Identify the action—the negative conditioned reaction—you want to change.

5. Intentionally shift your focus inward.

6. Sense the feeling in your body. Use awareness of your breath to locate the physical sensation of this feeling.

7. Experiment with your senses. Listen to the feeling, see if you can touch, smell, taste it.

8. Experience your inner feeling by breathing with the feeling.

9. Connect with your inner truth.

10. Experience inner joy.

Step 4: Breathe to the Inner Feeling

When you are aware of your breathing, you are not reacting. In steps two and three, experiencing yourself reacting and sensing the feeling within the body, you are becoming aware of your body breathing. The way you breathe is conditioned. Each of us has our own conditioned pattern of breathing. On the whole, people have forgotten about the power of breath, and forgotten how to breathe properly! Your body naturally breathes by filling your lungs with full diaphragmatic breaths. In my work with stress management, I often suggest to clients that they relearn how to breathe effectively. If you watch babies breathe as they are napping, their abdomen gently rises and falls. Babies' belly breathing in this manner is natural for humans of all ages, but instead of belly breathing, most of us breathe with our chest only, taking brief and shallow breaths using only a portion of the capacity of our lungs. We do not breathe in such a way that we fully fill the upper, middle, and lower lobes of our lungs.

Why? We are conditioned to believe that a flat stomach is good-looking, and so we learn to keep our center as tight and unmoving as possible. We have conditioned our bodies to breathe differently than the way the body needs to breathe. We are not breathing with our whole body. As we are not conscious of our breath, our breath operates for us on autopilot. We know we are breathing, but we are not aware of the breath as we breathe.

Take the time to become aware of your breathing. Sense your breath as it moves throughout your body. Listen to your breathing in quiet moments. This is important when dealing with your body's needs. During physically and mentally intense situations, people often hold their breath or take many quick, shallow breaths. To feel better, sometimes all you have to do is start to notice your irregular breathing, relax your belly and allow your body to breathe correctly. Belly breathing is highly therapeutic, and gets all the oxygen you need to your brain and other body parts. With awareness of your body breathing you can become truly aware.

Awareness of the Body Breathing

1. Sit down in a quiet space. Close your eyes and acknowledge a shifting of attention from your external surroundings and your thinking mind to the breath.

2. Focus your attention on the breath and become aware of your breathing.

3. Just allow your breathing to be whatever you feel at this moment.

4. When you have a rhythm that feels right for this time, begin to focus your breath on its passage in and out through the nose and mouth.

5. Sense the breath. Feeling the nostrils as the breath moves in and out through the nose.

6. Thoughts will break your attention and you will lose focus on the breath. As you take yourself back to the breath you are re-focusing your attention on the breath going in and out through the nose and mouth.

7. You may have the thought to breathe slower or deeper.

8. Simply return to the focus of your breath and find a breathing that is comfortable.

9. The breath is your entry into your body, and as you experience yourself breathing in and out you will find your attention follows the breath as you enter the body with the breath.

10. Allow your attention to follow your breath throughout your body, stopping wherever you experience a physical sensation. Breathe with the sensation.

11. With your attention on the breath within your body and experiencing your body breathing, invite yourself to experience the brain breathing, the heart breathing, the lungs breathing, the kidneys breathing, the liver breathing, the intestines breathing, the muscles and the bones breathing, and the skin breathing.

12. Your attention moves with the breath throughout the body and you are experiencing the body breathing.

When engaging this breathing exercise, do not try to get rid of thoughts. People are conditioned to focus on thought and not on breath. Just acknowledge your thoughts and return your focus to the breath. The experience of yourself breathing allows you to observe yourself consciously. As you become aware of your inner body, you are becoming the master of yourself—body, mind, and spirit.

When you are having a negative reaction, you are on autopilot, and not aware of your breath. When you are aware of our breath, you are conscious of yourself, your thoughts, your feelings and the impulse to engage a negative reaction. With awareness, you are able to consciously choose not to succumb to your conditioning. As you become aware of your body breathing, you are able to stop the negative reaction within yourself and de-condition yourself from having the unwanted response.

You will find that as you stay with the experience of your body breathing, bringing your attention back to the breath within the body each time your thoughts pull you away, a shift occurs in how you experience yourself. The shift is that you have moved from thinking, with cause-and-effect analyses going on in your head, to experiencing and being present and aware within the moment.

Whenever you choose to focus on your breathing, you can bring your awareness back to yourself in the present moment. And, as you go about your daily life, you will begin to notice that the quality of your present-moment awareness is directly affected by the quality of your body awareness. This is truly the key to excelling in life!

As you practice de-conditioning in your life and begin to experience yourself reacting, I encourage you to go to the breath and sense the feeling in the body as I describe above. Your impulse may be to share how you are feeling or why you are reacting the way you are, or to talk it through with the person to whom you are reacting. While this may be desirable at a later time, my advice is that while you are experiencing yourself reacting, you stop talking and go back to the breath. Sense the feeling in the body and breathe with the feeling. Once you feel balanced, your body will stop being on red alert and you will be fully present for any action or response needed in the situation.

As you Snap Out Of It—your conditioned thinking and inter-acting—Now! you are opening the door to your passions and inspirations. You are moving beyond what you once thought of as your traditional script. It's time to start feeling better; time to stop dreaming and go right to living your dream. It's time to be health-ier and happier, more centered and more successful—financially, physically, emotionally, and spiritually. It is time to embrace the inner joy that is your birthright! I love watching my clients snap out of it. I see realization in their eyes and suddenly they have a whole new life ahead of them. At that moment, they know it, I know it, and I promise you everyone who sees them knows it!

William James, an American psychologist of the nineteenth century, was asked at a meeting of the American Psychological Association to identify the most important finding of the first half-century of university research into the workings of the mind. He replied, "People by and large become what they think about them-selves." Now that you have begun to snap out of your subconscious negative thinking, you can lay the foundation for the reality you desire and consciously align your thoughts with what you truly want for yourself. Become your own conditioner by putting this into practice with the following journal exercise.

Snap Out of It Now! Moment

Becoming Your Own Conditioner

Make a list, either in your journal or right here in your book, of the all the positive aspects you want to begin seeing in yourself. Brainstorm with passionate, beautiful, joyful, abundant, and miraculous thinking. Pave the way for the experience you are looking for with good-feeling thoughts.

_____

_____

_____

_____

_____

_____

_____

_____

_____

As you hold the finest, most positive and healing thoughts toward yourself—body, mind, and spirit—you will prepare for the life experience that you are excitedly anticipating. Make your life everything you want it to be, in every way. You are so powerful: if your imagination can create an image, you have the power to become it! Allow yourself to be pulled onto your true path by your powerful and inspired new, joy-filled thinking. Blessings to you as you bring the best out in yourself.

Epilogue—Becoming Your Own Conditioner

When I sat down to begin writing, thoughts would enter my consciousness and it was then that I realized I could not write this book until I confronted the conditioning that was telling me, *I have no voice of worth.* I am happy to say that I have successfully done that, and it is my process, and what I have learned from my personal journey, that I am passing on here.

I wrote this book because I felt that I had to write this book—not to get rid of my fear of writing, and not to be free of the pain and agony that came when I thought that I could not write. I felt that had I not given myself fully to the process of writing to share my experience, the mystery within myself would die.

For as long as I can remember, I have wanted to understand life, God, Heaven, and the meaning of infinity. I remember at the age of 3 years feeling overwhelmed by questions in my own mind: *What happens when we die?* I thought, *We go to heaven, then what? What happens after heaven?* I did not know at the time that what I was trying to understand was what would happen to my consciousness.

Throughout my earlier years, I danced with the uncertainty of *how to be.* How to do the right thing. How to feel and how to think. How to express myself. How to participate with others, and respond to situations. How to experience myself, and how to experience others. I was aware that I wanted to be myself, but I didn't know how to achieve this. I remember having an awareness that I felt good when others were pleased with me and with the things I did, so I learned to be more pleasing to others, whether the things I did to please others agreed with me or not. Early on, I also realized that the more I did things that were pleasing to others, the more I denied and suppressed parts of myself.

Enveloped in uncertainty, I grew to believe that I was incapable of expressing my feelings and thoughts in an articulate and interesting manner. This belief continued to serve as an inhibiting factor in roughly every area of my life in those earlier years. As I continued to learn and grow as a person, I became capable of expressing myself with awareness and clarity, but never felt self-confident and continued to battle with feelings of low self-esteem.

Since that time, I have come to realize that the self-effacing belief was conditioned and inside I identified with it. As much as I wanted to say, "This really isn't me," my negative belief about myself had become a part of me. I eventually understood that my conditioning was my identity, and this conditioned identity was sabotaging and inhibiting me from believing in myself.

Many spiritual traditions assert that negative beliefs are simply thoughts that are not an intrinsic part of a person. However, from a psychological standpoint, they are. As long as you identify with your conditioning—subconscious thoughts, beliefs, actions and reactions—the only way to find your own voice and become your own conditioner is through acknowledgment of and confrontation with your conditioning. To see that my conditioning was not the true essence of me, I had to acknowledge that the conditioning was part of my perceived identity.

After I learned to live the life I wanted, I knew my mission was to help others achieve what I had. I became a psychologist, and I knew that I could offer my patients more solid support because of my own personal experiences with both the roadblocks and the triumphs in life.

I began my professional career with a large healthcare organization, but soon learned the limitations of working in a corporation. Excelling in this position called for me to move into a more administrative perspective, while simultaneously I wanted to do even more to help my patients, not less. I asked myself, *Is this the life I really want?*

As I confronted this question, my conditioning encouraged me to stay within the security of a job that I actually liked and where I was doing well. Yet, on a deeper level, I felt that in order to fulfill myself and my mission in life, I could not stay where I was. My work provided me with the opportunity to be effective in helping others, to have stimulating connections with colleagues, as well as a sense of respect and acknowledgment. But I felt it was time to stretch and challenge myself to help people more. So, I took a leap of faith, and made the decision to leave. I resigned my position and began my journey.

Then—*bam!*—I slammed face-first into the wall of my conditioning. The moment I took action to resign, my voice of conditioning rose to a shout, saying, *What do you think you're doing? You're leaving this security? You can't make it on your own. What will your family and friends think? What if . . .? What if . . .? What if . . .?*

How could I believe that I couldn't make it on my own when my intuitive voice was speaking so passionately about change and going forward in such a positive, quiet, and confident manner? Then I remembered something that I have always intuitively known. The true inner voice is the soft whisper that says, *Yes, this is it. Go for it. You can do it.* It never shouts or supports doubt in you. It may ask you to stop, look, and listen—to evaluate—but it will never send you in the wrong direction.

Clearly, the time had come to look at what I was proposing to do, and pause to listen to what voices were speaking to me. Once I had breathed to those voices, I felt clarity. I had what I have begun to call a Snap Out of It Now! moment. A moment when I had the opportunity to stop and take notice that I was about to slip into a conditioned reaction. In this moment I acknowledged the conditioning, breathed into the inner sensation provoking the impulse to react, and redirected my conditioning. By combining breathing exercises with my traditional Western psychological training, I was able to transcend to the next level of self-awareness.

In this way, I developed the Snap Out of It Now! method for people like myself, who have been conditioned from their earliest childhood in ways that neither they nor the people around them may have understood or acknowledged. A great deal of this conditioning becomes productive, good, and positive in our lives. Some is not, and these self-limiting perceptions and judgments have a negative impact on our lives.

The obstacles in your way are products of your own conditioning. You can learn to de-condition the reactions that keep you locked in the ways that are not working for you, just as I have. It has been an interesting road I have chosen to travel, and it all began because I was willing to stop, look, and listen—and breathe—then take action. To remain unaware of your conditioning is to live a life of repetition, cycling over and over through the many life patterns that do not work for you instead of embracing the joyous existence you so desire.

Snap Out of It Now! is a wake-up call to action. You cannot waste any more time.

By following the simple lessons in this book, you can learn to participate with your conditioning. You can become your own conditioner, and in this way you can create the life you want for yourself.

I did. And, so can you!

With an open heart,

Adrianne Ahern

Acknowledgments

Over the years that it has taken me to write this book, to find an agent and then a publisher, I have been thinking about the delight I will feel in being able to thank so many people for their support of me and my work. First and foremost I want to thank my husband, Barry Grundland, for his belief in me and his ability to maintain a calm, serene, and inspirational atmosphere in our home. I owe the wholeness of my life-my ability to become my own conditioner and thus follow my passion into the field of Performance Psychology-to your love, supportive guidance, and patient understanding.

I want to thank my mother, Joyce Ahern, for reading every word of the 400+ page manuscript, for giving honest, straightforward feedback, and for having the courage to read a book of self-discovery written by her daughter and love it.

Thank you to my beloved father and my brother Brendan in heaven, who continue to hold a place of deep love and inspiration in my heart. To my beautiful and brilliant siblings-Kevin and his wife Sherry, Patrick and his wife Laila, and Mary Kathleen-thank you for your love, loyalty, and ongoing encouragement during the most joyous of times as well as the darkest moments. To my beautiful nieces and nephews-Joseph, Trevor, Brianna, Brendan, Samantha, Garrett, and Harrison-thanks for being in my life. I send love to Daiden and Lauren-please know that I hold you both in my heart. To my 92-year-old Aunt Mary, all honor and gratitude for your love and prayers. You continue to be my ultimate role model. Thank you to Chad Carlsen for being such a strong and devoted father to my brother Brendan's granddaughter, and with his wife Kelly, providing a home full of love and joy. Thank you for bringing Aurora back into the heart of our family. A very special thanks to my darling great-niece Aurora, the source of so much happiness in my life.

I thank Almighty God for allowing me to belong to a very large and loving family, and I send the most tender thanks to the Ahern, Fischer, and Reeves families for all of their strong support and constant encouragement of me throughout my life.

Now, to those who do not share my home or my blood, the first person I want to thank is Dr. Judy Churchill, my professional mentor at ScrippsHealth and Mercy Hospitals. Thank you Judy for helping me reach the point of knowing the time had come to leave Scripps and begin creating my own work! I want to thank Dr. Richard Moss, my spiritual mentor and teacher, who helped open my eyes to my conditioned reality. And, thank you to the Hoffman Process for the gentle (maybe not so gentle, but loving nonetheless) nudge I experienced from the process to take the leap of faith and begin writing.

Thank you to all my supportive friends and helpers. To Renee Richetts for her loyal friendship and love, and Mary Jo Harte for her friendship, advice, and speech coaching. Thank you to Bernadette Doran, Ajah-Denise, Patricia Gonzales, Drew Boomer, Diane and Emily Tarpoff, Cindy Click, Peter Szollosi, Barry Krost, Bill and Barbara Bartolotta, Mike and Sally Elliman, Andy Katchen, Anne Sbicca Neffler, Martina Young, Emma Bezy, Gretchen Schodde and all of the wonderful women at Harmony Hill, Fanny O'Connor, Jan Usher, Emmy Moore Minister, Molly Zbojniewicz, Jenny Miles, Vicki Evans, Cami Lawrence, Clara Carrillo, Fu-Tung Cheng, and Shaun Farnsworth for bringing brightness, laughter, and kindness into my days of struggle with the book. Thank you Bridget Santos for your friendship and for modeling courageousness and perseverance in making this world a better place. Thank you to my childhood friends Carrie Morelan and her big sister Carolann Eddington for always showing their faith in me and never missing an opportunity for a good laugh! Thank you to Jane Senn for generously and willingly providing venues for my lectures and courses. Thank you to Patricia Kaye for your beautiful and encouraging words of wisdom in response to my e-newsletters. And, thank you to Gail Seminara at Transitions BookPlace in Chicago for your encouragement and joy of life! Thank you to all my friends and colleagues from Scripps and Mercy Hospitals, and a special thank you to Dr. Paul Randolph for always being available to support my work.

Thank you to my "India friends"-Arielle and Brian, Becky, Eileen, Suzen, Gloria, Divina and Mark, and our brilliantly creative leader Jai Varadarej. And to the priests at the sacred fire ceremony in Swamimalai who blessed *Snap Out Of It Now!* The memory of our time together in India, and our reunions since then continue to serve as inspiration and motivation to keep my vision alive.

Thank you Arielle Ford for your brilliant guidance in platform building, finding the right agent and hiring a top-notch PR firm-Wasabi Publicity. Thank you to the late John Austin who helped me to design and create my first website. And then to Mike Myers who kindly and compassionately took over for John after his sudden death. Thank you to Mike Koenigs and Vivian Glick for your brilliant and stimulating guidance with Internet marketing strategies.

Thank you Chad Edwards for all the hours we spent together in trimming words, sentences and pages from my original brain dump. And thank you to David Kraft-Schuttie for reading through each word of the manuscript, and for providing personal, honest and heartfelt feedback. Thank you Chad and David for believing in me.

Thank you to Joe Kulin and Parabola magazine for inviting me to do the commentary of a Parabola film, *In the Hands of Alchemy*, at the 1st Annual Spiritual Cinema Circle Film Festival-at-Sea. And, thank you to Jerry Wennstrom, author of *The Inspired Heart*, and his beautiful and creative wife Marilyn for having Barry and me to your home and allowing us to experience the truth and beauty of your life on Whidby Island.

To Janae Sigars-Molina, thank for opening your home to me and providing an opportunity to share my ideas and grow from the experience of being challenged.

Thank you to my SnapOutOfItNow.com online community who have consistently supported me and provided input into the design for the cover of *Snap Out Of It Now!* as well as each one of the CDs I created prior to the launch of this book.

Thank you to my agent, Bill Gladstone, for wasting no time with me and signing me within the first hour of meeting! This one event provided me with the confidence I needed at the time to keep moving forward. And, thank you Ming Russell for being available to me, believing in me, and generously offering such skillful guidance.

Thank you to my publisher, Connie Shaw, whom I now consider a friend. You have been an absolute joy to work with!

To Michelle Tennant and Drew Gerber at Wasabi Publicity and to all of their amazingly talented staff-thank you for all that you are doing for me in bringing my message to the world.

Thank you to Dr. George Pratt, Dr. Ken Druck, Dr. Judy Churchill, Dr. Alberto Hayek, Matthew Johnson, Linda Sivertson, and Jan Usher for your kind and generous offering of support in the form of an endorsement of this book. I appreciate it more than I can say.

Thank you James Arthur Ray for your wholehearted support of *Snap Out Of it Now!* How generous and selfless of you, at this very exciting and busy time in your own career, to take the time and write the foreword for this book. And, thank you to the glorious Tamika Catchings for providing your support through the second foreword of this book. I so appreciate the powerfully vulnerable sharing of your own experience and for encouraging others to see that *Snap Out Of It Now!* may help them transform their lives as you have intuitively done with your own life.

Sentient Publications, LLC publishes books on cultural creativity, experimental education, transformative spirituality, holistic health, new science, ecology, and other topics, approached from an integral viewpoint. Our authors are intensely interested in exploring the nature of life from fresh perspectives, addressing life's great questions, and fostering the full expression of the human potential. Sentient Publications' books arise from the spirit of inquiry and the richness of the inherent dialogue between writer and reader.

We are very interested in hearing from our readers. To direct suggestions or comments to us, or to be added to our mailing list, please contact:

SENTIENT PUBLICATIONS, LLC
1113 Spruce Street
Boulder, CO 80302
303-443-2188
contact@sentientpublications.com
www.sentientpublications.com

About the Author

Photo: Jeremiah Sullivan

ADRIANNE AHERN'S pioneering work in identifying and developing human potential began as she studied clinical psychology, earning two masters degrees and then her doctorate from the California School of Professional Psychology in Berkeley in the process.

Dr. Ahern lectures and leads workshops throughout the country on the Snap Out of It Now! method. This breakthrough methodology was developed over the last decade through her work with hundreds of clients, both in her own practice and in her consulting role at the prestigious Scripps Hospital in La Jolla, California.

During fifteen years of private practice, organizational consulting, and advanced research focusing on human athletic potential, Dr. Ahern developed these unique tools, which integrate the disciplines of psychology, psychophysiology, neurofeedback, and personal achievement analysis. Her clients and readers enjoy her simple, yet profound, strategies for bridging gaps between the heart, mind, and body, and use them to realize their goals.

Adrianne and her husband divide their time between Reno, Nevada and La Jolla, California. For more information visit her website, www.snapoutofitnow.com.